ISAIAH

Text copyright © Jo Bailey Wells 2006

The author asserts the moral right to be
identified as the author of this work

Published by
The Bible Reading Fellowship
First Floor, Elsfield Hall
15–17 Elsfield Way, Oxford OX2 8FG
Website: www.brf.org.uk

ISBN-10: 1 84101 151 7
ISBN-13: 978 1 84101 151 6

First published 2006
10 9 8 7 6 5 4 3 2 1 0

Acknowledgments
Scripture quotations taken from The New Revised Standard Version of the Bible,
Anglicized Edition, copyright © 1989, 1995 by the Division of Christian Education
of the National Council of the Churches of Christ in the United States of America,
are used by permission. All rights reserved.

Extracts from the Authorized Version of the Bible (The King James Bible), the rights
in which are vested in the Crown, are reproduced by permission of the Crown's
Patentee, Cambridge University Press.

A catalogue record for this book is available from the British Library

Printed in Singapore by Craft Print International Ltd

ISAIAH

THE PEOPLE'S
BIBLE COMMENTARY

JO BAILEY
WELLS

A BIBLE COMMENTARY FOR EVERY DAY

INTRODUCING THE
PEOPLE'S BIBLE COMMENTARY
SERIES

Congratulations! You are embarking on a voyage of discovery—or rediscovery. You may feel you know the Bible very well; you may never have turned its pages before. You may be looking for a fresh way of approaching daily Bible study; you may be searching for useful insights to share in a study group or from a pulpit.

The People's Bible Commentary (PBC) series is designed for all those who want to study the scriptures in a way that will warm the heart as well as instructing the mind. To help you, the series distils the best of scholarly insights into the straightforward language and devotional emphasis of Bible reading notes. Explanation of background material, and discussion of the original Greek and Hebrew, will always aim to be brief.

• If you have never really studied the Bible before, the series offers a serious yet accessible way in.

• If you help to lead a church study group, or are otherwise involved in regular preaching and teaching, you can find invaluable 'snapshots' of a Bible passage through the PBC approach.

• If you are a church worker or minister, burned out on the Bible, this series could help you recover the wonder of scripture.

Using a People's Bible Commentary

The series is designed for use alongside any version of the Bible. You may have your own favourite translation, but you might like to consider trying a different one in order to gain fresh perspectives on familiar passages.

Many Bible translations come in a range of editions, including study and reference editions that have concordances, various kinds of special index, maps and marginal notes. These can all prove helpful in studying the relevant passage. The Notes section at the back of each PBC volume provides space for you to write personal reflections, points to follow up, questions and comments.

Each People's Bible Commentary can be used on a daily basis, instead of Bible reading notes. Alternatively, it can be read straight through, or used as a resource book for insight into particular verses of the biblical book.

If you have enjoyed using this commentary and would like to progress further in Bible study, you will find details of other volumes in the series listed at the back, together with information about a special offer from BRF.

While it is important to deepen understanding of a given passage, this series always aims to engage both heart and mind in the study of the Bible. The scriptures point to our Lord himself and our task is to use them to build our relationship with him. When we read, let us do so prayerfully, slowly, reverently, expecting him to speak to our hearts.

PREFACE

At the heart of the Old Testament is the book of Isaiah; and at the heart of Isaiah is the gospel of God. If Isaiah is understood to fall into three sections—pre-exilic warnings, exilic assurances and post-exilic reconstruction—then it is the middle section that offers the key, reading it (as Christians do) with the benefit of hindsight. It addresses an exiled people who are desperate: the glorious past is undone, the present alienation is agony, and the future hope is dubious.

The tension between the reality of the people's rebellion and the promise of God's salvation holds the reader in suspense throughout the first part of Isaiah. How can it be resolved? But 'Second Isaiah' begins with comfort and relief. It is filled with assurances that the future is bigger than the past. Not only is God the Creator also God the Redeemer, but God who redeemed in the past, at the exodus, will redeem again. He will bring about a new exodus: he will rescue his people from their slavery once more.

Out of the tragedy of rebellion and exile, the next generation of God's chosen people recover a meaningful way to understand their story. Their pain may cause them to resist hearing God's voice of tenderness and his call to serve him, but God persists. He persists in promising salvation, enacted in the role of the Suffering Servant who fulfils Israel's mission to the world through obedient suffering and death in atonement. By 'absorbing' the old into himself, he delivers the new, even though the new things are glimpsed only partially at best. This is the Gospel of Isaiah, as I have come to perceive it.

The writing of this book has spanned a joyful time in my own life, with the birth of two children. But it has spanned a most painful period in the life of close friends through the breakdown of their marriage and its ripple effect on a whole community, especially on children. I have found the Gospel of Isaiah to speak to just such a situation. It offers a form of hope beyond denial, for individuals and communities in 'exile'—especially to the next generation who find themselves hampered by problems inherited from their parents.

This commentary is dedicated to the next generation—trusting that whatever the pain and chaos of your parents' lives, you will find hope in the saddened, deeply aggrieved potter-God, who tenderly scoops up the messy clay to create new vessels for his perfect ends (Isaiah 29:16; 45:9; 64:8).

I am grateful to those who have waited hopefully for this commentary during its gestation. Thanks are due to my husband Sam, who has helped create the freedom and focus with which to write, supported by our wonderful au pairs Jana Moravcova and Martina Rehakova. I'm grateful to students and colleagues at Ridley Hall, Cambridge, as well as Readers (lay preachers) in other parts of the country, who have welcomed me teaching with this material and responded constructively. I wish to thank friends for inspiration, some of whom even read the manuscript devotionally and pursued me with feedback: Deryn Coe, Kath Jourdan, Alastair Kirk, Sue Konzelmann, Joy Martin, Sue Walker and Helen Wood. And finally, my thanks go to those who steward the inspiring resources of Tyndale House—both human and literary—where the writing took form. Like the book of Isaiah itself, this commentary represents a shared enterprise.

Contents

	Introduction	13
1	Isaiah in a nutshell	24
2	Teenage rebellion	26
3	Fake religion	28
4	O Jerusalem!	30
5	'I have a dream…'	32
6	Pride and possibility	34
7	The Lord will take away	36
8	The great reversal	38
9	Unrequited love	40
10	God's plan	42
11	Seeking God	44
12	The harsh commission	46
13	Faith or fear	48
14	The sign of 'God with us'	50
15	But is God really with us?	52
16	Holy fear	54
17	Birth announcement	56
18	God's outstretched hand	58
19	God's rod of anger	60
20	Root and branch	62
21	The international signal	64
22	Songs of praise	66
23	World judgment	68
24	Concerning Babylon	70
25	Concerning Assyria and Philistia	72
26	Concerning Moab	74
27	Concerning Damascus, Israel, Judah and all nations	76
28	Concerning Ethiopia	78
29	Surprise… concerning Egypt	80
30	The wilderness of the sea	82
31	Concerning Jerusalem	84
32	Concerning Tyre	86

33	The broken covenant	88
34	Praising or pining?	90
35	A model for praise	92
36	Waiting and trusting	94
37	A new song of the vineyard	96
38	A precious cornerstone	98
39	In an instant	100
40	Rebellious children	102
41	This is the way; walk in it	104
42	Turn back!	106
43	The new king	108
44	Deliverance, again	110
45	Doom and desolation	112
46	Ransom and return	114
47	Sennacherib's intimidation	116
48	Hezekiah's trust	118
49	Sennacherib's fall	120
50	In sickness and in health	122
51	The word of the Lord is good	124
52	Here is your God	126
53	Lift up your eyes and see	128
54	Do not fear	130
55	My servant… my delight	132
56	A servant deaf and blind	134
57	And I love you	136
58	Do not dwell on the past	138
59	I will pour out my spirit	140
60	Return to me	142
61	Cyrus, the anointed shepherd	144
62	Every knee shall bow	146
63	Beasts of burden	148
64	Pride and fall in Babylon	150
65	Peace—but not for the wicked	152
66	Salvation to the ends of the earth	154
67	Forsaken and forgotten?	156

68	Weariness and wakefulness	158
69	In the shadow of God's hand	160
70	Wake up! Wake up!	162
71	The suffering servant (I)	164
72	The suffering servant (II)	166
73	Moving on	168
74	Come, see	170
75	Outsiders become insiders	172
76	Abiding evil	174
77	He whose name is holy	176
78	Seeking God	178
79	Sin, repentance and assurance	180
80	Gathering for glory	182
81	Transformation	184
82	A city not forsaken	186
83	God's vengeance	188
84	A psalm of lament	190
85	You did not answer	192
86	Fire and glory	194
	Glossary	196

PBC ISAIAH: INTRODUCTION

The book of the prophet Isaiah

The book

When Jesus read in the synagogue in Nazareth, he read from the prophet Isaiah (Luke 4:16–21). But he did not pick up a book—he unrolled a scroll. The whole 'book' of the prophet Isaiah would have been contained on scrolls, kept alongside scrolls of other prophets, written by hand and copied carefully but copiously so as to be available at each local synagogue.

Since then, much has changed. It is not just that Isaiah is widely available in printed form, translated into many languages and versions. It is now found in a fixed place next to other books of the prophets. These are placed within the Old Testament, which contains other literature—the Law and the Writings. Finally, the Old Testament is usually bound together with the New Testament to make what Christians call the Bible.

The Bible is one book, it is two books, and it is 66 books. For Christians, the Bible is one book, presenting the authoritative, final revelation of God. It is two books, in that the Old Testament and the New Testament belong together—the part that was written before Christ, and the part that was written after. And it is 66 books, in that the Old Testament is made up of 39 separate units, known as books, and the New Testament 27.

This commentary is a study of one of those 66 books, but because those 66 books are interrelated, quotations and ideas from Isaiah are found elsewhere in the Bible, just as parts of Isaiah are borrowed from earlier material. For that reason, in this study of the 'book' called 'Isaiah', I shall not confine myself to the book of Isaiah alone, but will seek to understand it in the context of the larger whole in which it now belongs.

The book of the prophet

A prophet had an established role in Israelite society. Deuteronomy describes the prophet as someone who speaks for God (18:15–18). God commissioned prophets in response to the request of the people who were scared of hearing God's voice face to face. So, from Moses onward, prophets acted as go-betweens, communicating God's message to his people. The Old Testament offers many examples of those who spoke on behalf of God to the people. Some of them have books named after them that record their prophecy—like Isaiah and Ezekiel—and others are simply described in other writings (such as Elijah and Elisha in the books of Kings).

Prophecy was a gift from God to Israel, but it was also a problem. How did you know if those who declared themselves to be prophets were really prophets? Whom could you trust? Scripture records some guidelines to help the people discern true prophecy from false (Deuteronomy 13:1–5; 18:20–22; Jeremiah 23:9–32; Micah 3:5–8).

The very fact that the record of certain prophets is included in the canon of the Bible indicates that those prophets were considered to be true prophets. So Christians understand that those who first heard the message of Isaiah discerned that God was speaking. Indeed, because of the way that God works through his word, people continue to hear God speak through Isaiah's message.

The book of the prophet Isaiah

Chapter 6 of Isaiah records the story of his call to be a prophet. He was in the temple—possibly, he was a priest—when a dramatic vision of God came to him. Out of it he heard God calling him to speak for him. God wanted to warn his people in Judah of the mess they were in, so that they could change their behaviour before the threatened judgment.

Because of the references to various kings, we know that this call took place in the sixth century, probably 741BC. This was a stormy period on the international front for Israel and Judah, and the early chapters of the book of Isaiah reflect the political tensions.

Later chapters, however, strike a completely different tone. Gone are the specific geographical and political references. Instead the material from Isaiah 40 onwards is more poetic and visionary, proclaiming hope rather than warning of disaster. Because of this contrast, scholars have conventionally assigned this material to a subsequent period and thus a different author. We refer to the section from chapter 40 to 55 as 'Second Isaiah' to reflect this change from 'First Isaiah' (chs. 1—39). The closing chapters of the book, 56 to 66 (which we call 'Third Isaiah'), are rather different again. Though more disparate in style, it is possible that these chapters stem from a later period still.

It is unlikely, therefore, in historical terms, that all the material in the book of Isaiah was delivered by a single prophet named Isaiah. The fact that the whole book is attributed to him, however, witnesses to the continuity of God's prophetic message that began with an original Isaiah and probably continued through other prophets dedicated to following in his footsteps. We might imagine a group of prophets who were called to continue Isaiah's work, even in a different era. Certainly, the book that now belongs in the Old Testament canon demonstrates thematic unity, despite the changes in period and style within the writing.

Issues in reading Isaiah

Why we read the Bible determines how we read the Bible. Over the 25 or so centuries that Isaiah has been heard or read, it has meant many different things to different people. The questions that readers bring to the text will determine, to a large extent, what they find within it. Below are some of the issues that have intrigued believers seeking to hear the book of Isaiah as God's word, all of which are pertinent to this commentary.

With regard to historical events

Prophecy involves a mixture of forth-telling and fore-telling, that is, speaking to current circumstances as well as predicting future circumstances. It is highly relevant, therefore, to explore the time and situation to which the message(s) of Isaiah might originally have referred—in order to work out what 'present' and 'future' events the prophet was addressing. In the early parts of Isaiah it is relatively easy to situate the material historically and geographically—given, for example, details describing the death of King Uzziah in Jerusalem (6:1, dated to 741BC) and the political crisis facing King Ahaz, concerning Syria and Ephram in coalition against Assyria (7:1–25). But this does not explain the whole of the book. For example, chapters 36—39 relate to a subsequent king, Hezekiah, 20 years or so after the downfall of Ephraim; and chapters 40 onwards appear to be situated in Babylon, not Jerusalem: they describe God's judgment of exile in the past rather than the future tense (see, for example, 40:2).

Scholars suppose, therefore, that the book of Isaiah stems from different periods of Israel's life: most commonly, eighth-century Jerusalem for chapters 1—39, sixth-century Babylon for chapters

40—55 and sixth-century Jerusalem (after the return from exile) for chapters 56—66. But even if we allow for these different historical settings within the one book, this does not resolve precisely how the prophecies about the future function. Does the situation of exile in 'Second Isaiah' (chs. 40—55) represent the fulfilment of the prophecies of judgment in 'First Isaiah' (chs. 1—39)? Similarly, does 'Third Isaiah' (chs. 56—66) represent the fulfilment of the prophecies of restoration in 'Second Isaiah'? To an extent, this is the case: the return from exile had fulfilled those prophecies geographically. Yet spiritually, the people were still waiting for the glorious promises of restoration to be fulfilled. Thus an expectation developed whereby the final 'layer' of fulfilment would take place at the end times.

Such tricky questions have been probed by modern scholarship using the tools of historical-critical analysis. While such analysis has been hugely helpful in reconstructing the possible history behind the text, it has tended to divide up the text itself into two or three parts that have then been studied and interpreted separately, losing any sense of their belonging together.

With regard to the story of Israel

The Old Testament is not only a resource for historians who are interested in uncovering 'what happened'. It is also a testimony to a relationship between God and his chosen people, which is itself a resource for that relationship. As in human relationships, there are ups and downs, and we must listen to many conversations to discern which are the important ones. But overall the Old Testament builds a theology by which to understand the ways of God, as well as the ways of his people.

In studying a particular book, therefore, it is relevant to find out where it fits into the wider picture. The prophecy of Isaiah presents God, through a prophet, re-calling his people to their foundational principles. It is as if they have forgotten that their very existence stems from God's promises to Abraham and the covenant he made with them at Sinai. There they made a commitment to listen to God's voice and obey his commands, while God invited them to be his priestly kingdom and his holy nation (Exodus 19:5–6). But Israel's life had drifted far from these expectations and privileges, and, having challenged them through many prophets, God was cross. Thus Isaiah warns that Israel may forfeit its status and its land —and be exiled.

The book of Isaiah as a whole gives the 'before, during and after' picture of exile. Studying Isaiah as a narrative in this way reveals many themes that run like threads through the whole work. There is, first, the picture of God in his holiness who is sovereign over all creation; second, the reminder of his plan for all nations through Israel; and third, the language of God as transforming potter, creating and recreating his people as if handling clay. Such 'narrative' approaches to the book of Isaiah draw attention to the continuities that exist within the book, even if it falls into three differing sections.

With regard to Christ

It is as if Matthew sat on the shoulders of Isaiah when writing his Gospel. Isaiah is cited in the New Testament more often than any other Old Testament book. Because it promises the Messiah (chs. 9 and 11) and explains the death of a suffering servant (ch. 53), it is seen both to predict and explain the work of Christ. It foreshadows his life and his death. Isaiah has been regarded, therefore, as a 'fifth' Gospel.

Without questioning the process by which these prophecies of Isaiah became drawn on to the person of Christ, it is important to remember that they first carried significance long before they were identified with Christ. Christians need to look behind their 'Christian' interpretation, if only to recover more fully what it means to say that Christ took upon himself the whole destiny of Israel and acted out the Gospel of Isaiah as if it were his script. It is valuable, therefore, to explore what the prophecies might have meant before Christ, before recognizing what they have come to mean in the years AD. This underlines the many 'layers' of fulfilment to Isaiah's prophecies, which Christians find to culminate in Christ.

With regard to the Church

In the process of interpreting Isaiah, Christians cannot rest once they have drawn the connections between the promises of Isaiah and the person of Christ. Just as the role of the individual servant reinforced Israel's call to be a servant, so, for Christians, an understanding of Christ as servant functions to reinforce the call of Christ to serve (like him) on behalf of the world. What Jesus did for Israel, so the Church is called to do for the world—if the Church is to be the body of Christ and serve God's plan of salvation for all. It is not enough to make connections between the Old Testament exile and its ending in Christ, for Jesus' own life and work, understood through the lens of Isaiah, makes a call upon the Church. The Church is God's new people, his means to continue ending exile and bringing healing to the world all around. Just as Israel did not exist for its own sake, but as an instrument of God's plan to the world, so it is with the Church. Salvation is not so much God's gift *to* the Church, as God's gift *through* the Church to the world.

Further reading

Shorter commentaries

Walter Brueggemann, *Isaiah 1—39* and *Isaiah 40—66* (Two vols; Westminster Bible Companion), Westminster John Knox, 1998

John Goldingay, *Isaiah* (New International Bible Commentary), Hendrickson/Paternoster, 2001

Alec Motyer, *Isaiah* (Tyndale Old Testament Commentaries), IVP, 1999

J.D.W. Watts, *Isaiah* (WBT), Word, 1989

More detailed commentaries

Brevard S. Childs, *Isaiah* (Old Testament Library), SCM/Westminster John Knox, 2001

R.E. Clements, *Isaiah 1—39* (New Century Bible), Eerdmans and Marshall, Morgan & Scott, 1980

Paul D. Hanson, *Isaiah 40—66* (Interpretation), John Knox, 1995

Otto Kaiser, *Isaiah 1—12* (Old Testament Library), SCM, 1983

Otto Kaiser, *Isaiah 13—39* (Old Testament Library), SCM, 1980

Peter D. Miscall, *Isaiah*, JSOT Press, 1993

Alec Motyer, *The Prophecy of Isaiah: An Introduction and Commentary*, IVP, 1993

J. Muilenburg, 'The Book of Isaiah, Chapters 40—66', Introduction and Exegesis in *The Interpreter's Bible* (vol. 5), Abingdon Press, 1956

John N. Oswalt, *The Book of Isaiah: Chapters 1—39* and *The Book of Isaiah: Chapters 40—66* (NICOT), Eerdmans, 1986 & 1998

Christopher R. Seitz, *Isaiah 1—39* (Interpretation), John Knox, 1993

David Stacey, *Isaiah 1—39*, Epworth, 1993

Marvin Sweeney, *Isaiah 1—39*, Eerdmans, 1996

J.D.W. Watts, *Isaiah 1—33* and *Isaiah 34—66* (WBC), Word, 1985 & 1987

C. Westermann, *Isaiah 40—66* (Old Testament Library), SCM, 1969

H. Wildberger, *Isaiah 1—12: A Commentary* (Continental Commentary Series), Augsburg/Fortress, 1991

H. Wildberger, *Isaiah 13—27* (Continental Commentary Series), Fortress, 1997

Time chart

Date BC	Characters	Events
2000–1500?	Abraham, Isaac, Jacob, Joseph	Events of Genesis 12—50
1300–1200?	Moses	Events of the 'exodus'
1200–1000?	Israelite tribes settle in Canaan	Events of Joshua, Judges
1030–1000?	King Saul	The monarchy is established
1000–970?	King David	The 'glory' years
970–932	King Solomon	Building of the temple
932–916	King Rehoboam	Division of the kingdom into Israel (north) and Judah (south)
916–914	King Abijah	(Following the southern line of kings)
914–874	King Asa	
874–850	King Jehoshaphat	Political alliance of Israel and Judah, sealed by marriage between the two royal houses
850–843	King Jehoram	
843–842	King Ahaziah	
842–836	King Athaliah	
836–797	King Joash	
797–769	King Amaziah	
769–741	King Uzziah	

Events referred to in First Isaiah

741	Isaiah	Vision of God in temple
741–734	King Jotham	Assyrian empire grows under Tiglath-Pileser III (745–727)
734–715	King Ahaz	War with Syria and Ephraim (Israel) Israel falls to Assyria (722)
715–697	King Hezekiah	Sennacherib (King of Assyria) invades Judah (701), but Jerusalem is saved

697–642	King Manasseh	Assyrian empire wanes
642–640	King Josiah	Law code discovered in temple; period of reform. Prophecy of Jeremiah
609	King Jehoahaz	Babylonian empire grows
609–598	King Jehoiakim	Babylon defeats Egypt (605). Nebuchadnezzar invades Judah
598	King Jehoiachin	First deportation to Babylon
598–587	King Zedekiah	Destruction of temple. Second, more prominent, deportation to Babylon. Prophecy of Ezekiel

Events referred to in Second Isaiah

571		Jehoiachin released from prison in Babylon
556	Cyrus king of Persia	
539		Cyrus captures Babylon

Events referred to in Third Isaiah

538		Cyrus' edict allows return of exiles
537		First group of exiles return under Sheshbazzar
520–515	Darius king of Persia	Prophecies of Haggai and Zechariah
515	Zerubbabel governor; Joshua high priest	Second temple is completed

458		Ezra arrives in Jerusalem
445–432	Nehemiah is governor	
400–300?		Editing of Chronicles, Ezra, Nehemiah
331		Alexander the Great conquers the Persian empire

Map 1: Ancient cities and nations relating to the prophecy of Isaiah

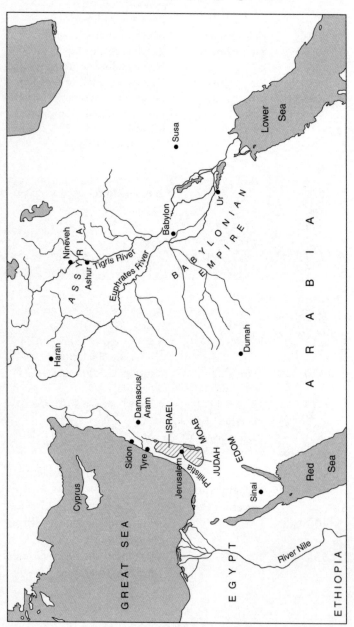

Map 2: Corresponding modern cities and countries

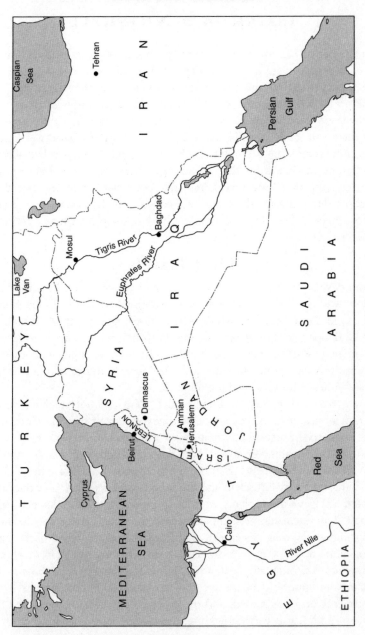

1   THE BOOK OF ISAIAH

Isaiah *in a* Nutshell

In the period that we now know to be about 700 years before Christ, God's people were in a bad way. They used to live in a plentiful promised land, but now that land was divided, and the largest area, to the north, was under threat. They used to be twelve united tribes but now there were two in the south who refused to be allied with the ten in the north. They looked back to a glorious era when David was king, but now their kings seemed to be far from good. What was left of the kingdom was far from safe or strong. There was an imbalance in society: the rich were prospering; the poor were suffering. But the people did still have their precious capital city, Jerusalem, and their most precious building, the temple. This was the place where, through sacrifice, God took away their sins.

First Isaiah

One day, Isaiah went into the temple, and he saw God. He saw that God was holy. He knew that God wanted his people to be holy, like God himself, and the whole world to be holy through the holiness of God's people. But Isaiah saw that both he and his people were far from holy. Rather, they were sinful, and God was angry with them. Even the king was not serving God. Having seen things in a new way, Isaiah offered to do something about it.

He told the people and their king, 'You are not fulfilling your covenant promises to live for God so that you may be holy like God and be his special possession. If you don't want to be like God, God will take away everything from you, even your land and your temple. It will be like a deep darkness.' Even though God gave them future hope in a vision for the new Jerusalem and the promise of a messiah, they did not listen. He gave them plenty of time to repent, but little changed, so, about 150 years after he had first warned them, and after many further warnings, they were besieged by Babylonian armies (598BC). God sent the nation over 600 miles away, to Babylon. This was not far from where Abraham had originally come from, Ur: it was like going backwards in history and undoing the 'progress' of the past 1000 or more years. The promised land was ruined, and the precious city of Jerusalem razed to the ground. It was very depressing; these were dark times indeed.

Second Isaiah

In Babylon, they felt even smaller than before, and even more surrounded by other nations. It was a struggle to remain faithful to God when they were oppressed by their captors and tempted by false gods. But in Babylon God spoke again. The people's understanding of what God was like, and what it meant to be holy, changed. God announced that he was no longer angry; rather he revealed his compassion and care. He called his people to be his once again, and they realized afresh how much he loved them. He reminded the people that he created the heavens and the earth—that nothing was beyond his power. Thus the place of exile became a place for transformation and hope. After nearly 50 years in Babylon, God used a different foreign nation—the Persians, led by Cyrus—to rescue his people and restore them to Jerusalem (538/7BC).

So they made the long journey back home. Their hope had turned to joy: they knew what it was to be given a second chance. And they understood what it meant to serve their God. They began once again to rebuild the city of Jerusalem and rebuild the temple. For the second time, they were given the promised land.

Third Isaiah

But the returned people became anxious: rebuilding their community and realizing the vision for the new Jerusalem did not prove as straightforward as they had hoped (537–515BC). They argued about who should care for the needy and on what terms foreigners should be welcomed. They were even disappointed with God, and impatient with their progress towards renewal and re-creation. They were reminded: 'You will show God your joy by the way you care for the neediest people in your country, and by the way you invite other nations into the holiness and company of God.' Meanwhile they had to wait for the day of fulfilment, for the final dawning of light into the darkness. God's work—of judgment and restoration—was not yet complete.

REFLECTION

*With which stage do you identify most readily: a people being
warned, feeling displaced or returning home? Do you look for the
possibility of God's transformation throughout times of prosperity,
adversity and rehabilitation?*

2

ISAIAH 1:1–9

TEENAGE REBELLION

Isaiah's opening verses are hard-hitting. There is already a serious problem for God's people (vv. 2–4) and it is about to get worse (vv. 5–9). The mention of Sodom and Gomorrah (v. 9)—tales of God's judgment recounted since the time of Abraham (Genesis 19)—evoke fears of God's fury to send shivers down the spine.

Isaiah's introductory vision is anchored to a particular time and place (v. 1). The four named kings ruled in Judah from about 740 to 690BC (see time chart, p. 19). King Uzziah had a long and prosperous reign, during which Isaiah's ministry as a prophet first began (see 6:1). Jotham's reign is less significant for Isaiah. King Ahaz follows, about whom Isaiah has more to say (see 7:1–17) because he is weak and fails to trust God. And after him comes his promising son, King Hezekiah, on whom the hopes of the nation are pinned (Isaiah 36—39).

The first vision concerns Judah (the southern kingdom) and the focus is on its chief city, Jerusalem. This is the royal city of David, and the holy city of Zion. It is as if God's majestic reign and his powerful presence are somehow contained within its walls.

Rebellious children

Yet God is found issuing a charge, as if in a law court, to which all heaven and earth are called as witnesses (v. 2). It is a matter of cosmic concern that God's precious children have rebelled against him. Despite God having been a caring, nurturing parent (compare Hosea 11:1), the children have run away, pretending that they don't even know him. Even the ox and the donkey—animals not renowned for their intelligence—know better.

Verse 3 refers to the children by name: they are 'Israel', that is, the people God liberated from slavery in Egypt. These are the children he carried through the Red Sea when they were in danger. These are the children he fed in the desert when they were hungry. These are the children he invited to seal a special covenant relationship with him and to be called his treasured possession, when they promised to obey him and keep the law (Exodus 19:1–8).

But now that treasured possession lives as if it does not know God. Verse 4 begins with the parent's desperate cry—'Alas!'—and continues

26

with the full range of vocabulary for the sin that follows from abandoning God's ways. Israel's covenant name for their parent, YHWH (see Glossary, p. 198), is used, underlining the scale of the tragedy, and the unique title 'the Holy One of Israel' then echoes throughout the book of Isaiah. YHWH alone is 'the Holy One', and he has invested that holiness in Israel. In forsaking and abandoning their God, the people of Israel are 'utterly estranged' (v. 4; literally, they have 'bestranged themselves backwards'). Their alienation is not something that God has done to Israel but what Israel has brought upon itself. As Deuteronomy 27—30 puts it, to live in covenant with God is to experience blessing, but to break the covenant is to experience curse.

Rebels in the hands of God

Now Isaiah warns that Israel lies in danger of making things worse (v. 5). The head and heart are so sick that Israel can't stop on this path of self-destruction. The people are caught up in some kind of masochistic addiction: why would the nation choose yet more punishment when the wounds still bleed (v. 6)? Beyond the alienation of the people lies the alienation of their land. The same term for estrangement that described the Israelites in relation to God (v. 4) is now used of 'strangers' who invade the land (v. 7). Judah will be devastated: looted and ransacked by foreigners. Only 'daughter Zion'—the city of Jerusalem—will remain, standing exposed on a hill with the land levelled all around, like some lonesome shed propped up in an abandoned vegetable patch (v. 8). Thus Judah is likened to Sodom and Gomorrah: God's beloved holy people are associated with the rudest, crudest name imaginable. They are to suffer at the hands of the God who has become their adversary, now titled 'YHWH of hosts' (the God of the troops, v. 9). The only ray of hope is that, unlike in his dealings with Sodom and Gomorrah, God will at least spare a remnant.

Verse 1 invites the reader to relate these events to the massive devastation of Judah caused by the Assyrian invasion in 701BC. Yet the wider context of Isaiah points beyond this crisis to a further, more serious devastation by the Babylonians. Could it be that foreign nations are instruments in the hands of Israel's God, executing punishment on his wayward children so as to enable his wider purposes in the world?

PRAYER

Lord, help me to feel your pain when we, your children, rebel.

3

FAKE RELIGION

In terms of their physical danger, Israel is *like* Sodom and Gomorrah
(v. 9), but now verse 10 declares that, in terms of their spiritual
state, they *are* Sodom and Gomorrah. Initially Israel's problem was
described in terms of ignorance and stupidity. Now, as the camera
focuses more closely, we see a situation that is more wilful and more
serious. The problem, essentially, is about dishonesty.

Vain worship

Both leaders and people need to heed God's word and God's teaching (v. 10). Even though they seem to observe the regular activities
of worship prescribed in God's law—with sacrifice, burnt offerings,
fattened animals and the blood of bulls, lambs and goats (v. 11)—
God says that he rejects them. He doesn't want them even to set
foot in his temple (v. 12). Not only are the priestly offerings futile; the
community gatherings are also offensive (v. 13). God hates the seas-
onal festivals and sabbath observance too (v. 14). It is as if Isaiah
catalogues every 'religious' activity, and roundly condemns them all.

The purpose of worship is to sustain a relationship with God.
Central to the Israelite system of worship is the practice of sacrifice,
offered by priests in the temple. This is the God-given way to deal
with sin and so to restore the relationship when something goes
wrong. Prior to the sacrifice of Christ, it is the means by which the
people can express penitence and receive forgiveness.

The irony of the situation in Judah is that, far from sustaining a
relationship with God, their worship is undermining it—it is insincere, which makes God weary. Their sacrifice is not restoring a
wrong: it *is* the wrong. And, in case the people are prone to blame
their priests, or the institution they serve, even the outstretched
hands and the prayers of the congregation are compromised (v. 15).
Dishonesty and insincerity are all-pervasive throughout Israel.

It is a typical feature of the Old Testament prophets of Isaiah's time
to condemn the ceremonial aspects of worship (see, for example,
Amos 5:22-24; Micah 6:6-8), but the problem of outward observance versus inward attitude is familiar to Christians today just as to
eighth-century Israelites. At best, the outward and inward aspects

belong together and sustain each other. Sometimes, however, the external, more measurable practices of religion are maintained when the invisible, more subtle dispositions and attitudes have dwindled or disappeared. It is often easier to go to church than to love one's neighbour. Yet it is vital that the gestures of worship represent a devotion to living the whole of life for God—or else they undermine any serious relationship, and Jesus called this hypocrisy (Matthew 23:28).

The way back to God

Isaiah cannot be accused of being wholly negative. In contrast to the comprehensive and repetitive critique of Israel's worship in verses 10–15, verses 16 and 17 present a brief series of urgent imperatives to spell out the way forward. Cumbersome language is replaced by relative simplicity. First, Israel must deal with the past and replace evil with good: 'wash... be clean... remove... cease'. Second, Israel must pursue a different path in the future: 'Learn... seek... rescue... defend... plead'.

Israel is urged to set about some intentional change and to take responsibility for the situation. It is not simply that high-brow religious activity should be replaced by the down-to-earth pursuit of social justice, that the 'priestly' be replaced by the 'prophetic' (as some Protestant commentators choose to read it). 'Washing' probably refers to ritual cleansing, which, like baptism, depends on repentance as well as symbolic ceremony. Rather, it is that honest religion extends to all of life, including the relationships we might overlook. A change of attitude will be revealed by practical action. Thus, real repentance for the past will show itself in a concern for the less fortunate in the future. 'The oppressed, the orphan and the widow' (v. 17) are a common trio, representing all who are subject to political, social or economic exclusion. Thus the people are urged to pursue holiness *and* justice. Both are aspects of the character of the God whom they worship, and whom they are called to imitate.

PRAYER

Lord, help us not to rely on outward show; make us clean within.

O JERUSALEM!

Verse 21 marks the beginning of a lament, which is typical of prophetic language. The lament focuses on the city of Jerusalem, the city that represents the nation as a whole and encapsulates the promises of their God. But O... 'how the faithful city has become a whore!' Hear the cry of pain in God's voice! Whatever Jerusalem used to be, whatever she might be if she would repent, she has now become the centre of Israel's problems. If another city were the centre of rebellion and wickedness, that would be bad. In Jerusalem, it is catastrophic.

How it once was

The language of God as parent (1:2) has changed to that of God as husband, and rational argument has moved to more emotional expression. God committed himself to Jerusalem in love and faithfulness, but she has deserted him for other lovers. She has diverted her attentions and gifts elsewhere. It is not just that the one who invested everything has been spurned: the sovereign has been 'upstaged', replaced. Where justice and righteousness used to dwell, there are now prostitutes and murderers (v. 21). The pure has become impure; the precious has been debased (v. 22). Care of the widow and the orphan has been replaced by self-interest and greed (v. 23).

God mourns the loss, and the dross. The previous declaration of judgment now becomes an expression of grief. God is angry, but also he is sad. He bestowed everything, but has now been scorned.

Therefore...

This situation has dire consequences that are spelled out in verses 24–26. On the negative side, the beloved has become the enemy, the foe—thus the focus of God's anger and the target for his retaliation (v. 24). Looking at it more positively, God's action will be constructive: the damage will be reversed. The silver that was cheapened by an impure mix of metals will be purified by fire (v. 25). God's overall purpose is not devastation but restoration, and not just of the leaders (who are the prime rebels, v. 23) but of the city as a whole. Once again, Jerusalem will be described as faithful (v. 26).

Afterwards

Beyond the punishment there is hope. The cloud that hangs over Jerusalem will have a silver lining. This is no easy hope: it is not a way out of suffering. Rather, it is a post-suffering hope: 'Afterwards you shall be called the city of righteousness, the faithful city' (v. 26). As 1:8 suggested, at the end of the trials that lie ahead there will be some survivors—those who repent (v. 27).

When will this 'afterwards' happen? Unlike the historical references that begin Isaiah's vision (1:1), here there are no strings with which to tie down the rays of hope. Judah and its people are under threat and trouble is on its way, and they are urged to hang in there—because there will be an 'afterwards'. But when?

As readers who come to Isaiah with the benefit of hindsight, we sit in a privileged position. We may identify the slim survival of Zion 'like a shelter in a cucumber field' (1:8) as, first of all, a reference to the Assyrian invasion. This took place during Hezekiah's reign (701BC), when much of Judah was devastated but Jerusalem survived. The larger scope of the chapter predicts gloom for Jerusalem as well, however. With further hindsight, this could be identified with the total devastation of the southern kingdom at the hands of the Babylonians (597–593BC), when Israel was carried off into exile. These two different moments of historical reference illustrate the many layers in Isaiah. The fulfilment of the prophecy is not necessarily limited to a single situation in history.

What of restoration? Under the Persians, in 537BC, Israel was offered the opportunity to return from exile. Verses 27–28 describe a sharp division in Zion, between the righteous and the rebels. The ends of these two groups will be quite different, even though, for the time being, they may co-exist side-by-side.

Christians recognize a further layer here. Indeed, the restored (yet desolate) Israelites found themselves still anticipating the promised salvation of Zion long after the official return from exile—since Jerusalem needed rebuilding and enemies continued to threaten. Thus the hoped-for restoration became an eschatological hope, projected further into the future. It was into this situation that Jesus came. His parable of the wheat and tares (Matthew 13:24–30) speaks of the co-existence of the righteous and the rebels in the kingdom of God until the very last day.

REFLECTION

God is for ever optimistic. Are you?

5   ISAIAH 2:1–5

'I HAVE *a* DREAM...'

Preaching in the USA in the 1960s, Martin Luther King Jr borrowed a technique from Isaiah. He presented his dream of racial equality in just the manner that Isaiah presents a vision of international peace. Despite superpowers that threaten Israel from the outside, and faithless living that undermines Israel from the inside, Isaiah's vision declares that Jerusalem has a golden future.

The mountain-top

The prophet presents, literally, a mountain-top experience. People from all nations will gather on this highest mountain to worship God. Isaiah is imagining a completely new order of religious relations (with God) and international relations (with one another). The world will no longer consist of rival powers and gathering armies. Rather, there will be a harmony of purpose and a justice concerning difference. There will be peace-making instead of war-mongering, and there will be a devotion to the God of Jacob and his ways.

It is said that the United Nations established a similar vision of peace and justice when it was first formed after World War II. The horrors of war were so recent that the determination to prevent any future war was very great. Thus new ways for nations to relate to each other were conceived so as to overcome the causes of war. A new era of justice and righteousness was surely near!

Isaiah's vision conceives new ways for nations to relate, but this is a by-product and not the chief concern. The governing council is not a delicate representation of leaders determined by certain countries united by a common pact: it is the Lord, YHWH. The God of Jacob is also the Lord of all.

Here is a reminder to a wayward people that their God is the God of all nations. His ambitions lie far beyond the simple sorting out of Judah and Jerusalem described in chapter 1, but sort them out he will, for their holy city Jerusalem is his chosen dwelling place. The mountain of the Lord's house will be raised above all hills (v. 1). It will be the place where all peoples, not just Israel, will gather to meet; and they will migrate here not just to meet each other, but to meet God.

After the predicament of Judah and Jerusalem introduced in chapter 1, surely this vision comes as a surprise. Here is some good news to follow the bad news. Yet, more fundamentally, this vision is far from a surprise. Rather, it articulates again Israel's most basic tradition.

Blessing to all the families of the earth

Abraham is the one to whom God first revealed his plans. Genesis 12:1–3 tells how God singled out 'Abram' from all peoples and nations, and invested in him and his descendants the intention of blessing for the world. God promised that Abraham would be blessed and that he, in turn, would be a blessing—not just to his direct descendants but, through them, to all the families of the earth.

Israel owed its very existence to this foundational promise. In this promise, therefore, Israel found its identity and calling: to embrace God's blessing and, in turn, to be a channel of that blessing to the rest of the world. Isaiah's vision paints a picture of that promise working out, of the nations streaming to Zion where God's blessing is found.

In days to come

This vision, therefore, constitutes a reminder to Israel. It is not surprising, perhaps, that Israel had lost track of the larger picture, given its more immediate problems, but in the face of dangers and threats Israel cannot afford to forget its privileges and responsibilities. This is the people whom God has chosen to be pivotal for all people.

If Israel longs, therefore, for others to learn of God's ways and walk in his paths (v. 3), how absolutely vital it is that the people return again to embrace God's blessing and live by it. The days to come will not arrive until God's instruction—his covenant Torah—flows out of Zion again. If other peoples will one day say, 'Come, let us go up to the mountain of the Lord', then Israel must first 'come', and 'walk in the light of the Lord' (v. 5).

REFLECTION

The 'days to come' have begun—they started when people of all nations were gathered in Jerusalem at Pentecost and the Church began to teach the ways of her God through Christ.
Do you seek to bring about this vision?

PRIDE & POSSIBILITY

The first part of chapter 2 is a thrilling vision of the future reality. The second part is a disturbing analysis of the present reality. The contrast could barely be greater. The house of Jacob, urged to walk in the light of the Lord (2:5) and reclaim its distinctive destiny, is now 'outed'. The people of Jacob have forsaken those ways (v. 6). They have so welcomed foreigners that they have 'clasped hands' with them and abandoned their unique covenant identity. Indeed, their land is described as full of alternative practices—as if there is no room for walking with God.

The land is full of diviners and soothsayers, offering religion without responsibility. The land is full of silver and gold, suggesting a wealth-based, not welfare-based economy. The land is full of horses and chariots, implying the acquisition of weapons to win power by force. And the land is full of idols—presumably, along with money and weapons, the 'fullness' of self-security and self-congratulation. This aggressive consumer society is encumbered with affluence and bloated with pride; and, much like the Tower of Babel (Genesis 11), its lofty self-image is a false construct.

How the mighty are fallen...

That which flaunts itself as fullness is, in fact, emptiness; that which masquerades as lofty is base. A refrain develops through verses 10, 11 and 17 that declares how the haughty will be humbled and every-one brought low. Indeed, the fall will be so great that Israel will be reduced to dust. Worse still, their covenant God, YHWH, will be-come 'YHWH of hosts', a fearful military enemy who stands against them (v. 12). Like David hiding from Saul in the cave (1 Samuel 24)—or Saddam Hussein hiding from his would-be captors in the ground—so Israel will hide from their God (vv. 10, 19, 21). The future promise of peace and harmony is lost, for the moment, in humiliation and terror. For the Lord alone will be exalted. The problem is not about foreign influence so much as the betrayal of God's absolute glory and majesty.

Isaiah asserts God's sovereign authority over his people. This is not a message that God has abandoned them: it is that they have abandoned God. The flip side of his coming salvation is his coming judgment. God will not abandon his people; and because he will not abandon them, he will bring about justice. 'In that day' he will visit them and be exalted among them. God's justice necessarily turns an indulgent, self-confident society upside-down. The ten objects that God stands against in verses 12–16 all describe figures of pride and self-sufficiency. The cedars of Lebanon and oaks of Bashan are symbols of strength; the high towers and fortified walls are references to royal prestige; the ships and beautiful craft epitomize achievement and affluence. All this will pass away (v. 18). Indeed, as people run for cover, they will end up throwing the treasures they tried to bring with them to moles and to bats (v. 20)!

The seeds of change

This prophetic critique issues a challenge to any affluent society about the dangers of complacency and idolatry. It is hard to live for God alone in a situation—ancient or modern—where there is so much choice and comfort and competition. Indeed, it is hard, faced with greed fed by free enterprise, and anxiety exacerbated by power, to stand back and imagine things differently. Just as the words of Isaiah may originally have addressed a post-Yahwistic context in the eighth century BC, so they continue to challenge a post-Christian context in the 21st century AD.

Walter Brueggemann argues for the power of such rhetoric to fire the imagination. It is through powerful poetry such as that of Isaiah 2—a reminder of God's glorious plan, as well as a challenge to contemporary culture—that we are empowered to help bring about social change. And this is the charge that is incumbent upon all who inherit the prophecy, all who assign ultimate authority to God.

It was, perhaps, just this rhetoric that enabled Mary, overjoyed at the prospect of giving birth to God's Messiah, to recognize God's plan in action and to reassert its familiar topsy-turvy themes.

REFLECTION

He has scattered the proud in the imagination of their hearts,
he has put down the mighty from their thrones, and exalted those
of low degree; he has filled the hungry with good things,
and the rich he has sent empty away.

Luke 1:51–53 (RSV)

7

The LORD WILL TAKE AWAY

This chapter presents a situation of chaos in Judah and Jerusalem when YHWH 'takes away' (3:1, 18). As in chapter 2, the scenario is an imagined one, a description of what may be and what will be, given the predicament of God's people. Things are going to get worse. A picture builds of despair and disgrace.

At the outset, God takes away 'support and staff'. Elsewhere, God is described as Israel's support and staff (for example, Psalm 18:18). Here the loss is depicted first in terms of bread and water, the most essential elements of sustenance (3:1). It then extends to include a range of leadership roles: military, religious and political (vv. 2–3). The 'starvation' of society spreads, such that the established roles of parent and child, old and young, neighbour and relative, are thrown into turmoil (vv. 4–6). The vacuum of leadership leads to a dismantling of anything that represents a reliable framework for civil life. No one will take responsibility, everyone gets desperate (v. 7), and anarchy ensues. The downward spiral is such that there is no longer even a semblance of respectability; defiance is blatant (vv. 8–9). Thus the people can no longer bring themselves to look God in the eye: the poetry alludes to their 'faces' (v. 9) far removed from God's glorious 'eyes' (v. 8, AV).

Responsibility and judgment

The calamity began with God 'taking away' sustenance, but the disaster is the logical outcome of the actions of the people (vv. 9, 11), especially the leaders (v. 12). It is not that all the people are guilty: some are innocent (v. 10), whose deeds are quite different from the rest. Here, perhaps, is a further reference to that vulnerable 'booth in a vineyard', the shed in the vegetable patch (1:8): the scarce survivors who form a remnant (1:9; 4:2; 6:13; 10:20–21).

In verses 13–15 YHWH takes centre-stage: he 'stands up' and declares his judgment in no uncertain terms, but on which 'peoples'? Usually this term is used of foreigners, but suddenly the camera zooms in and focuses on 'his people', in particular on the leaders (v. 14). Feel the shock, the glare, the shame! 'It is you who have devoured the vineyard; the spoil of the poor is in your houses.' The social analysis is familiar and chilling: God's concern lies with the poor and vulnerable, and his anger lies with the powerful and wealthy. This note of judgment hints again at a reversal: those responsible for 'grinding the face of the poor' (v. 15) are those heading for a humiliating change of fortune. And, by implication, perhaps those who are currently crushed are those who will constitute the remnant?

Daughters of Zion

In the final section of this indictment, the threat of judgment moves from one social élite, which is largely male—the elders and princes— to another élite, constituted by 'high society' women. These people are depicted strutting around like peacocks, flaunting their finery with heads held high. The juxtaposition of verses 15 and 16—the poor with faces in the dust compared to these women tottering above it all—speaks for itself. It is not just those invested with authority who are held to account for injustice: included also are those who capitalize on class distinctions and delight in conspicuous extravagance. For these people, the reversal will be even more abrupt and public: the coiffure will give way to scabs and baldness; the robes will give way to rags and nakedness (vv. 17, 24). Those who are not widows now will become widows (3:25; 4:1). As at the beginning of the chapter, here again it is the Lord who will 'take away' in that day (v. 18).

This material is designed to offend, to pierce the resistance of even the most complacent. The offence is targeted at particular groups, defined by gender or class or role, but is not limited to those sections of society. For anyone in the city who does not feel vulnerable now is destined to 'lament and mourn; ravaged... (to) sit upon the ground' (v. 26). No one is safe, and those who seem safest are, in fact, those most at risk. God's judgment involves his 'taking away' the rug from under their feet.

REFLECTION

What offends you in this text—the public humiliation of celebrities or the private oppression of the poor? God's judgment brings a reversal. Is this good news or bad news for you?

8   ISAIAH 4:2–6

The GREAT REVERSAL

Throughout the previous section of Isaiah, the phrase 'in that day' (also translated 'on that day') has prompted God's unrelenting judgment of his wayward people (3:7, 18; 4:1). It comes again here, but this time there is relief. It announces good news: the other side of punishment is restoration. It reaffirms God's judgment as God's great reversal. This feature is underlined by the reappearance of many motifs from the previous section.

The branch of YHWH (v. 2) recalls the cedars and oaks of 2:13, whose lofty heights required felling, and the vineyard of 3:14 that was devoured. But here is a shoot that, unlike its associates, grows and flourishes to produce fruit once again. The branch is beautiful, replacing the so-called beauty of the daughters of Zion (3:24). Its fruitfulness echoes that of the innocent (3:10), and fosters pride—replacing the pride of the haughty (2:11, 17; 3.16). The survivors are described as those left in Zion and remaining in Jerusalem (v. 3), recalling the image of the booth left over in the vineyard and the shed remaining in the cucumber field (1:8–9). There is a reversal for the daughters of Zion, when their humiliation is washed away, and those who previously hid from the terror and glory of YHWH (2:10, 19, 21) are now protected by that glory as if by a canopy.

The description of restoration also brings together some foundational themes. The notion of a pillar of cloud by day and of fire by night (v. 5) alludes to Israel's experience of exodus and their journey through the wilderness. God's presence was visible there, and his protection palpable. It was this pillar that brought them to Mount Sinai to meet with him. Here God invited his people to enter into a covenant relationship with him, with the consequence that they would be a holy people (Exodus 19:6). This was a calling that Israel constantly failed to live up to; yet here, in verse 3, those who are left in Jerusalem are called holy. It is a thrilling claim.

A tapestry

These few verses, addressing the other side of judgment, weave a remarkable picture: they combine past and present, making sense of both God's calling and Israel's failing. The warp—the strong vertical threads—consists of the long-term promises. These form the main-stays, given by God, across which are woven the shorter loose ends of recent experience, as weft. The result is a picture of restoration, a tapestry that makes sense when viewed standing back. The restored Jerusalem is not discontinuous with what came before; indeed, it fulfils what was previously incomplete. At the same time, the restoration does not ignore or deny Israel's failures: the reversal somehow makes them good, turning problems and weaknesses into the material of grace and possibility. The new creation, though ultimately larger, is thus made from the leftovers—the remnants—of the old.

And when is that day?

Scholars commonly attribute the message of impending doom to the 'original' prophet of the eighth century, and assign these more hopeful words to a later editor. This assumes that, with the benefit of post-exilic hindsight, the editor peppered the long chapters of gloom with slivers of hope, based on God's subsequent gift of restoration.

Whether or not this is so, the message of Isaiah (as it now stands) presents an ongoing threat of judgment coupled with the ongoing possibility of restoration, matching the pattern that Judah and Jerusalem experienced in the period before, during and after exile. Words originally addressed to a particular period and people are now afforded a wider application—not least to Christians, as well as to successive generations of Israelites.

This suggests that although God is already understood to have acted in history according to the manner described 'in that day', his promised reversal is not yet complete. This was the experience of Mary (see p. 35). Also, for those Israelites who did return from exile, their hopes were not matched by their experience, causing them to look to the future for the fulfilment of God's restoration. Thus this tapestry is open to new viewing—and, perhaps, to further weaving. The greater the distance from which we view it, the better we may see the bigger picture that emerges. For example, we may wish to revisit 'the branch of YHWH' (v. 2) in the light of subsequent texts and see here (as in 11:1) messianic overtones.

REFLECTION

What does the tapestry of your life look like? What have been the threads of judgment… of restoration… and of hope?

UNREQUITED LOVE

Here is a love song, which Isaiah begins to sing to Judah and Jerusalem on behalf of God. It is as if the prophet had been best man at the wedding of God and his people, and now, at a point of crisis in the marriage, he reminds them how it once was.

This offers a new perspective on the same sad state of affairs in Judah and Jerusalem. Far from the parent dealing with an ungrateful child, or the sovereign who is offered false worship, or the ruler who presides over anarchy (as in recent chapters), here is God presented as a lover. It is a heart-rending picture of pain. This conventional image of courtship (found also in the Song of Songs) describes how he gave his beloved everything: his best vineyard, and his devotion to cultivate it and guard it and make wine in it. But it was not appreciated—as if there was never even a 'thank you'. The lover feels snubbed: God is heartbroken. After the first two verses, God's own voice breaks into the song in desperation. As if with the strains of a violin playing in the background, we hear the forlorn cry, 'What more was there to do for my vineyard that I have not done?' (v. 4).

Wild grapes

The lover had hoped for a reward for his labour of love: the yield of some good grapes. Fruitfulness does not seem an unreasonable request of vines, especially of those that receive the very best tender loving care. Indeed, the whole purpose of cultivating vines is to produce grapes! This vineyard produced only wild grapes, however (vv. 2, 4): sour and scrawny little offerings that defied all the attention God lavished on them. Such grapes do not make wine.

As Isaiah 1:8 implied, this vineyard is destined for destruction. The flip side of God's extreme love is his extreme anger at the betrayal of that love. As passionately as God earlier dug, cleared, planted, built and hewed (v. 2), so in due course he will remove, break, lay waste, and command drought (vv. 5–6). We have already heard warnings about God 'taking away' (3:1—4:1). Without the vine keeper, the vineyard becomes as wild as the grapes it was already producing.

The lover had expectations of his beloved that were not fulfilled (vv. 2, 4): he believed in them and hoped they might respond according to their immense potential and his single-minded devotion. They failed to meet these expectations (v. 7), which put the marriage—the covenant relationship—in jeopardy. The expectations had been clear in the initial invitation for Israel to enter into covenant with God (Exodus 19:3–6). It was an invitation to mutual relationship, like a marriage, involving commitment on both sides, but Israel had reneged on its pledge: Israel was not 'fruitful'. God was unable to reap the harvest he had sown. The outcome was disappointment, distress and 'divorce'.

Fruitfulness

The metaphors are explained directly in verse 7. The vineyard is the house of Israel and the vine is the people of Judah. As for fruitfulness, God 'expected justice, but saw bloodshed; righteousness, but heard a cry!' The Hebrew here offers some evocative wordplay to draw a shocking contrast between the expectation and the reality. The terms for justice (*mishpat*) and bloodshed (*mishpakh*), as for righteousness (*tsedaqah*) and outcry (*tse'aqah*), sound very similar, yet the behaviour could not be more different. Justice and righteousness denote positive social relations, marked by equality and generosity rather than abuse or exploitation. Yet the reality consists of outpouring and outcry: the bleeding of the poor and the protest of helpless victims.

Jesus adopts the same images of vineyard, vines and fruitfulness in the Gospels. In the parable of the tenants (Matthew 21:33–46; Mark 12:1–12; Luke 20:9–19), it is God's abiding concern for gathering the fruit that brings him to send servants—and eventually his son—to collect it, despite the dangers. The paramount importance of the owner's receiving his crop is understood by his hearers (Matthew 21:41). In John 15, Jesus uses the image of a vine to explain his relationship with the Father and with his disciples. Again, the purpose of growth and the criterion for pruning is, throughout, fruitfulness. The figure of good fruit represents, variously, the product of a godly life (Matthew 3:8; 7:16–20) or virtues of character (Galatians 5:22–23; Ephesians 5:9; Philippians 1:11). But always this fruitfulness is the outcome of obedience (John 15:10–11) and the evidence of salvation (John 15:2, 4; Hebrews 6:9).

REFLECTION

Read the passage again, and hear God singing this love song to you.

10   ISAIAH 5:8–30

GOD'S PLAN

The first few chapters of Isaiah have been building, inexorably, to the pronouncement of God's judgment. Despite the interruption of two hopeful visions (2:1–5; 4:2–6), the momentum of these opening chapters is clear: Judah is heading for disaster.

The disaster is now spelt out categorically. God's people will be exiled (v. 13), and a foreign nation will invade (vv. 26–30). It will happen, speedily and efficiently, at YHWH's bidding (v. 26). Like a lion seizing its prey, the invaders will carry the people off to a place beyond rescue (v. 29). Suddenly cosmological punishment takes on historical particularity: the transcendent threat becomes savagely concrete, with political and geographical ramifications. Just as previous chapters warned and future chapters will repeat (9:12, 17, 21; 10:4), God's anger is kindled and his arm is stretched out against his people (v. 25). He means it! The tense in which these events are described is that of past fact or future certainty (the same Hebrew tense encompasses both possibilities).

Crisis? What crisis?

Rather than focusing on the style and language of this declaration, it is appropriate first to consider the historical circumstances that surround it. To what was this prophecy understood to refer, and when did it 'come true'? The 'nation far away' (v. 26) is not named. Firstly, addressed to a late eighth-century audience in Jerusalem, the reference is associated with Assyria (see also 10:5–19; 36:1—37:38). Assyria was to ravish almost all of Judah before the eighth century was out, leaving Jerusalem exposed but intact. Those who read the book of Isaiah with hindsight are invited, secondly, to identify the foreign invader with Babylon. It was the Babylonians who, in 587, eventually destroyed Jerusalem and forced the Israelites into exile (see 39:5–7). Finally, there remains a future aspect. 'In that day' (v. 30) has eschatological overtones, suggesting that judgment extends beyond Israelite history into a cosmological dimension. Thus it now stands to warn of judgment for any and all time, following the pattern experienced with Assyria and Babylon. Further threats to God's people are possible—or even likely—if their life departs from God's intention, if they reject

YHWH's instruction (v. 24). God's people are not automatically safe: his love and his promises do not constitute the protection of an insurance policy. Rather, in circumstances of economic exploitation (vv. 8–9, 23), self-indulgence (vv. 11–12, 22) or distortion (vv. 18–21), where there is injustice and unrighteousness, God's justice and righteousness rise to the fore (v. 16) and prove dangerous.

According to plan

Isaiah makes absolutely clear what lies ahead. The prophet's point is stressed by the taunt of the Israelites themselves: in verse 19 they mock, 'Let the plan of the Holy One of Israel hasten to fulfilment, that we may know it!' The irony here brings one to laugh and cry: since he first began, Isaiah has been speaking to them of God's plan and warning them that it is hastening to fulfilment. They have clearly not listened or understood, however, or they would not welcome it so blithely! This illustrates beautifully the point of the previous verses: all the feasting and merriment has numbed their senses to what God is doing (v. 12).

The notion of God's plan introduced here is an important idea in Isaiah. It is found in all three sections of the book, underlining their theological continuity as well as the overall nature of God's purposes. The whole book of Isaiah affirms (as do the Israelites in their reference to it here in verse 19) that God's ultimate plan is for blessing. But this picture does not preclude a more immediate reference: God's plan involves the destruction of Judah. Although this is alien to God's ultimate nature and purpose, it will be done if necessary as a means to achieving the original, wider intention, just as the gardener prunes the vine (5:1–6). Nothing, ultimately, can prevent God's blessing, even when God's people prove counterproductive towards the unfolding of that plan.

Judah and Jerusalem are indeed counterproductive. When the judgment happens, it is as if God's creation is partially undone: the roaring of the sea and the darkness over the land (v. 30) are reminiscent of the early stages of the account of creation in Genesis 1. There is a partial return to chaos, as at the flood (Genesis 6—9), and primordial sadness.

PRAYER

Lord, please hasten your plan of blessing.

SEEKING GOD

Here is the most important part of the book of Isaiah. Isaiah has an experience of the holiness and the glory of God. This vision becomes the basis for Isaiah's life and work. It also becomes the basis for the unfolding of the rest of the book named after him.

This passage is often described as Isaiah's 'call'. As a call narrative, it is compared to other accounts in the Old Testament where God calls a person to be his prophet. As with those of Jeremiah and Ezekiel, the account usually comes at the very beginning of the prophetic book, giving the prophet's background—their 'qualifications' for the task—so a prophet's authority is established and the message reinforced from the very start. This one is different. The account of Isaiah's calling tells us more about God than about Isaiah.

Holy, holy, holy

Isaiah is worshipping in the temple, as usual, when he receives a vision of the glory of the holy God filling the whole earth (v. 3). God is awesome in majesty, enthroned on high and surrounded by seraphs who are worshipping him continuously (vv. 1–2). Their cry, 'Holy, holy, holy' is (in Hebrew) the strongest possible way to express God's supreme and overwhelming quality of holiness.

What does God's holiness mean? The portrayal of God we are given here continually stresses the sovereignty of God. He is a God of matchless power, a king who rules over all nations and whose glory cannot be contained. At his voice, buildings tremble and people fear. Even the seraphs must hide their faces from him. We might expect, then, that Isaiah will feel small and scared as he glimpses the king, overcome by his own powerlessness in the face of God's overwhelming majesty.

Isaiah is overwhelmed, but for a different reason. He is overwhelmed by a sense of his own moral unworthiness in comparison to God's absolute purity. He is suddenly aware of all that is ugly and profane within himself and, equally, within the world (v. 5). Far from feeling paralysed or being complacent at such a moment, Isaiah pleads for mercy on behalf of himself and his people.

Isaiah repents, and the seraphs touch his lips with burning coals from the altar. This practice recalls the system of temple sacrifice: a burnt offering is made in the holy of holies, so that sin is forgiven. Isaiah is restored in spirit. As he is forgiven, so is he inspired and empowered for God's service.

Isaiah as representative for Israel

From this perspective, Isaiah realizes immediately that it is the failure of himself and of the people generally to reflect the sovereignty of God that accounts for their decline from prosperity to desolation. The 'unclean lips' that characterize Isaiah characterize Israel also (v. 5). Isaiah now demonstrates the proper response to the recognition of God's holiness: that of worship.

Isaiah is humbled, in contrast to the haughty (5:15). He draws near to understand the purpose of the Holy One (unlike those who are exiled for want of knowledge, 1:4; 5:13, 19). He responds with the offer of faithful obedience, in contrast to those who have been faithless and disobedient. He offers to act on God's behalf, and so fulfil a purpose within God's plan. So the personal response of Isaiah models that which is demanded of all God's people (compare 8:18): repentance, worship and service.

A vision and a call

It is significant that the 'call narrative' in Isaiah does not open the book that is named after the prophet, as it does in Jeremiah and Ezekiel. It is not Isaiah's personal authority that is the basis for receiving the message of Isaiah; it is the glimpse of the character of God that is the basis for the book. The vision of God's holiness explains God's complaint with his people, outlined so far in chapters 1—5, and it explains both his judgment and his salvation of Israel throughout the rest of the book.

PRAYER

Grant, holy God, that as I embrace the message of Isaiah, I too may glimpse your holiness, know your forgiveness and fulfil your call; for the sake of your kingdom and your glory.

12   ISAIAH 6:8–13

The HARSH COMMISSION

Looking more carefully at this supposed 'call narrative', we discover that it is not exactly a call. Rather, in response to the vision, Isaiah makes an offer (v. 8). Isaiah's vision of the Lord is so powerful and so penetrating that it brings him, on the one hand, to a sense of his unworthiness in God's sight and, on the other, to a sense of his importance for God's plan. Rather than being asked—and far from being collared—Isaiah offers himself for service. He declares himself ready for despatch.

This offer is presented as the obvious, logical reaction to Isaiah's new understanding of God (as, indeed, is the message that follows, according to John 12:41). He has glimpsed God's holiness, and, far from signalling his end, it has brought about forgiveness and a new beginning. The implication, of course, is that if the people of God were fully to realize God's holiness—his incomparability, his moral purity and his sovereign grace—then they might realize their problem and ask for God's mercy.

Let sense be dumb

As things stand, it seems that there is no chance of the people seeing what Isaiah has just seen, for God seems to demand that Isaiah close down their senses so as to prevent them from noticing and turning to be healed. The message is harsh (v. 9), and the task scandalous (v. 10). Does God really desire to harden people's hearts? These two verses have sometimes been interpreted as a prediction, speaking of what would happen (as in, for example, Matthew 13:14–15; Acts 28:26–27). Certainly, the rebellion is so serious and the pride so great that Isaiah finds people oblivious to the truth.

But this is not just about prediction; it is also about intention. It is not just about the hearers; it is also about God. Verse 10 suggests that God does not want them to see or understand or be healed (this is the sense of the quotations in Mark 4:12; Luke 8:9; John 12:39–41). Yet, in previous chapters, Isaiah has already expressed God's longing for Judah and Jerusalem to look and listen and comprehend, to turn and be healed. Here, then, is an announcement that it is now getting late. It is designed to shock, for judgment is nigh! And God's 'intention' is, in fact, only a confirmation of the entrenched intention of the people. By denying any problem and continually ignoring the message, they are bringing judgment on themselves (3:9; 5:12–13, 19).

Isaiah's preaching in the chapters that follow confirms this. He does not merely repeat verse 9 literally—he keeps on trying to bring people to their senses so that they may indeed turn and be healed—but he meets exactly the response it describes. It is the same in the Gospels when these words are repeated in reference to Jesus. Those who do not properly understand and receive him are asking for judgment, and this judgment is seen not just as the logic of wilful hardheartedness but as the outcome of the will of God. The purposes of God include judgment in particular circumstances—for the ultimate sake of healing and salvation in a wider, universal context.

This difficult 'hardening' passage from Isaiah is found in each of the Gospels, stressing how Christ's preaching continues the selfsame struggle of God with Israel found throughout the Old Testament. Indeed, the rejection and crucifixion of Jesus were the ultimate climax to a pattern that extended throughout Israel's history (see Acts 7) and has continued in the Church.

Distant hope

Isaiah's complaint, 'How long, O Lord?' (v. 11), expresses his distress at this commission. He echoes the standard cry of lament (see, for example, Psalm 13:1–2) to plead for mercy. The answer only confirms the coming devastation and exile (vv. 11–12), until the mysterious words at the end. The notion of an old tree cut down and burnt, even as a stump, underlines the declaration of unrelenting judgment. But in that remaining stump, under a pile of dead wood, there hides a real twinkle of hope: a holy seed, waiting to sprout. This does not refer to a lucky group who escape judgment. It is about those who emerge from 'death' to rebuild life thereafter. The mystery of Israel is about the death of the old and rebirth of the new. It is to this enduring mystery that Paul testifies in Romans 11:1–12: God has not ultimately rejected his people, despite the dreadful reality of judgment.

REFLECTION

Echo for yourself Isaiah's cry of lament, 'How long, O Lord?' Feel the same pain as you reflect on all that brings God's judgment.

FAITH *or* FEAR

These verses mark a change of direction after chapters 1—6. Chapters 7—8 address the particular circumstances of an acute political crisis that faces King Ahaz, described elsewhere in 2 Kings 16:5–9. Judah's two closest neighbours to the north, Israel and Aram (Syria), have joined forces and threaten Jerusalem. In a panic—his heart shaking 'as the trees of the forest shake before the wind' (v. 2)—Ahaz looks for help to the massive empire of Assyria even further north.

The house of David

Ahaz has lost the plot. He is searching for military security, and is consumed with practical worries. Imagine the king of Judah checking out Jerusalem's plumbing (v. 3)! He has lost the theological perspective invested uniquely in him as representative of the 'house of David'. The assertion of this title (v. 2) recalls God's promise of unconditional loyalty to David's line (described in 2 Samuel 7:11–16). Yet Ahaz is not trusting in the security of God: he is acting, rather, to undermine that security. His political manoeuvring makes him more like the kings of Aram and Israel than a king in the line of David.

Isaiah is instructed to go and meet Ahaz with his son (v. 3). The boy's name carries a symbolism that is powerfully ambiguous. *Shear yashub* means 'a remnant will return'. On the one hand, this speaks of the remnant of Assyria who will return if Ahaz trusts God. On the other hand, it points to the remnant of Judah who will return to their land—following exile—if not. An innocuous child thus presents Ahaz with a far-reaching choice, but can this Davidic inheritor be shaken from fear and summoned to faith? The scene of foolishness is almost comic, like the tale of the emperor who has no clothes and the boy who dares to say so.

No faith... no future

In conventional prophetic style, Isaiah speaks on behalf of God (vv. 4–9). His message is practical and reassuring. This is not a serious political crisis, although it is in danger of becoming a serious faith crisis. The king does not need to panic, but he does need to trust. The prophet can see this situation for what it is: the two northern nations are mere 'smouldering stumps' (v. 4), whereas Ahaz, blinded by fear, has lost a sense of proportion.

The poetry of the last line of the oracle is worthy of special attention: 'If you do not stand firm in faith, you shall not stand at all' (v. 9). The same Hebrew verb for trusting, maintaining faith, being reliable and committed—used also of the faithfulness of God to the house of David (2 Samuel 7:16; Psalm 89:24)—is used in each phrase. There is a pun between its active and passive sense. Those who rely on the promises of Yahweh have a future that is reliable. Those with *faith* are those who '*stayth*'. An equivalent might be a bumper sticker: 'No faith... no future.' The message to Ahaz is simple: there is only one source of true assurance and well-being—not Assyria, but God.

This challenge informs the whole message of Isaiah. Those who receive the prophecy of Isaiah in its present written form, with the perspective of the preceding chapters, know that the exile is already certain. This scenario with Ahaz gives just one example of a whole nation who failed to trust God. With hindsight, therefore, the name of Isaiah's son may also offer a symbol of hope—at least a remnant will return—despite the tragedy of Ahaz' course. For Ahaz did not heed Isaiah's warning. Although his alliance with Assyria brought short-term relief, it bore incalculable long-term consequences.

God's word to Ahaz regarding faith has thus become God's word to all subsequent generations too. This faith is not about the intellectual details of belief. Highlighted by a situation of vulnerability and weakness, faith is about the practical action of trusting God. The opposite is not unbelief or doubt, but fear. To those who find such faith a risk, this text demonstrates the greater risk of trusting in Assyria rather than in God. In due time, military might or strategic allies will prove less reliable. Contrary to appearances, those who stand secure are not those with power or popularity, but those who recall the promises of God and cling to them. Scripture testifies to this truth again and again, from Abraham and Moses, to Jonah and Daniel, to Peter and Paul.

PRAYER

Lord, grant me the security that can only be found in a deep and abiding faith in you—in the knowledge that your promises are true.

The SIGN of 'GOD WITH US'

What begins as a word of comfort for King Ahaz becomes a word of warning in verses 10–17. It is followed by a second oracle addressed to Judah more generally (vv. 18–25). Both continue to address the crisis of faith brought about by the threat to Judah of the northern alliance of Syria and Israel.

A sign to Ahaz

How does one get through to someone who is losing their head in panic? God has reassured Ahaz on a personal level with words of comfort: 'do not fear' (7:4). He has also reassured him on a professional level with a political analysis of the situation: 'it shall not come to pass' (7:7). But to no effect. Now there is a further gesture of reassurance: he offers Ahaz a sign—just as he offered Moses, for the purpose of fostering trust (Exodus 4:1–18).

Ahaz rejects the sign. Belying his pious quotation from Deuteronomy 6:16 in verse 12 is a defensive retort from a person who will avoid trusting God whatever the evidence. This resolute act of unfaith becomes final. It marks the turning point in the fortunes of the house of David, and the sign of hope becomes a sign of warning.

The sign is that of the birth of a baby. We are not told who this child is (see further comment on 8:1–4, p. 52). The identity is not what matters here. By the time this child has grown sufficiently to distinguish nice food from nasty food (perhaps as a toddler aged 2 or 3), he will be enjoying curds and honey. These are symbols of prosperity, suggesting that the threat from the north will have passed and everything will return to normal—'God with us'—once again. But the sign of hope became a sign of warning: within three years both Israel and Syria had been plundered.

The very name Immanuel, 'God with us', underlines the deeper problem for Ahaz, who categorically refuses 'God with him'. The problem is spelt out suddenly in verse 17. Further ahead lies big trouble for Judah, trouble that is comparable only with the tragedy of 922BC when the kingdom divided and Ephraim (Israel) split from Judah—and this is to do with the king of Assyria! The one whom Ahaz now befriends for defence will become his oppressor.

A sign beyond Ahaz

The sign that is given to Ahaz has become, in Christian tradition, famously associated with the birth of Jesus. The reinterpretation of verse 14 in Matthew 1:23 is aided by the Greek version of the original Hebrew text, which translates 'young woman' as 'virgin'.

So, the very sign that, to Ahaz, signalled God's abandonment of the line of David has become, in God's due time, a messianic sign of God's remembering the house of David. The sign was fulfilled in its most immediate sense when the dynasty collapsed following the reign of Hezekiah, Ahaz's son. In another sense, the sign of Immanuel, 'God with us', remained unfulfilled amid the realities of exile and occupation. A sign that had turned into a sign of warning for Ahaz became, once again, a sign of hope for the generations suffering thereafter.

Thus the Christian interpretation of this sign represents a subsequent, and ultimate, fulfilment. Humanly speaking, the dynasty of David had ended, but God brings about a restoration through the divine–human Messiah. Although the link with the promises to Mary and Joseph has become normal—if not 'natural'—within Christian tradition, we should not overlook that this is a miraculous provision, demonstrated through a miraculous birth. And, as before, the presence of a transcendent and holy God with us brings both weal and woe, blessing and curse—according to the way he is received.

No faith... no future

The remainder of the chapter (vv. 18–25) illustrates just how grim the coming days will be, as the land reverts to wilderness. The wider context (especially 9:1–7 and 11:1–16) suggests that this theme penetrates the apocalyptic realm. Surely, we may ponder, Ahaz could not have known the far-reaching consequences of his actions, or he might have acted differently. If he were to embrace 'God with us', then he could welcome both the warnings and the promise of this sign. He refuses, however, preferring 'God away from us' to 'God with us'—as if that were possible.

REFLECTION

How does God's gift of the sign 'God with us' impact you?

15

But Is God Really With Us?

God tells Isaiah to find a huge billboard and write his message in bold letters, so that everyone can see it. If 7:10–17 can be understood as a sign and explication directed personally to the king, then here is the sign presented to the people.

Parallel texts

The message is remarkably similar, even down to the birth of a baby. As before, the prophetic word is delivered through the naming of this child—a kind of visual aid—which makes absolutely clear what God is doing. Again, the message is one of warning: the name (a wordplay on 5:19) speaks of unambiguous defeat. As in 7:15–16, by the time the child is a certain age (before he develops the language skills for 'Mummy' and 'Daddy') Samaria and Damascus will cease to be a threat to Judah because they will be defeated by Assyria (v. 4). As previously when the king rejected God's word (7:2, 14, 17), so the people's refusal is explicit (v. 6) and devastating. The water supply that Ahaz was so keen to protect (7:3) becomes the very symbol of 'overwhelming' in verses 6–8. The normal steady trickle swells to Euphrates proportions under Assyrian influence and becomes a mighty flood, drowning Judah up to its neck. Owing to their failure to trust, the people are powerless. But there is hope: Judah is only engulfed as far as the neck, not annihilated completely. The promise of 'God with us' recurs (vv. 8, 10).

The mystery of a child

As often happens with poetic parallelism, the second unit goes beyond the first. Both the structure and the themes of chapter 7 recur, but there is greater intensity. This underlines the most bewildering (if also elusive) element. Somehow, a child incarnates this coming judgment. The link is mysterious, yet firm.

Who is the child? In chapter 7 the description was enigmatic, leaving open several possible candidates. Scholars argue variously for different interpretations. Was the child Hezekiah, the son of Ahaz who followed his father on to the royal throne? Certainly he represents the answer to Ahaz: cast as the model of obedience, replacing his father's archetypal failure, and thus renewing the faith and hope of a nation and saving Jerusalem. This seems most likely, except that the dating in 2 Kings would suggest that he was already a young boy at the time of this prophecy. Was the child, rather, the son of Isaiah and a brother to Shear-jashub (7:3)? This interpretation adds a certain symmetry to the context. In contrast to the historical search for a particular boy, however, are those interpreters who suggest that the child is a representative figure—a kind of A.N. Other. The prophet need not have a particular 'young woman' in mind, but any Israelite woman who would marry and conceive in the normal way, whose child would still be young by the time disaster struck. Yet others argue that it did not refer to anyone before Jesus.

The last suggestion is unlikely, given the historical basis of prophecy. True prophecy was that which proved relevant and was found to be fulfilled within its given context. Any of the other three suggestions are feasible, but the first would seem most obvious. The presentation of King Hezekiah later in Isaiah 36—39 bears this out. The parallel birth of Isaiah's son, therefore, emphasizes to the people the sign that God gave to Ahaz. Through the 'innocent' appearance of a child, God announces doom for Judah as well as allowing, somehow, for the possibility of hope beyond. The doom is sure, and coming soon, whereas the hope is still mysterious. We only know that it is associated with the name Immanuel, not least by the dual repetition of this name from 7:14 in verses 8 and 10.

How can God be with us?

The immediate force of the message about judgment begs this question—the question of all who suffer: 'How can God be with us in such horrific circumstances?' The people have been 'asking' for it as a result of their behaviour, and God urges them to change and avert the crisis. Beyond this, he 'appoints' the king of Assyria to function as his agent (7:17, 20; 8:4, 7). Although God may declare that he is 'with' Judah, as Immanuel, so in another sense he is 'with' the enemy—working through a self-serving, power-hungry foreigner who ransacks Judah.

REFLECTION

*Do you recognize God's child-like vulnerability with you
in times of suffering?*

HOLY FEAR

The upheaval of a military crisis brings not just political analysis, the prediction of outcomes and 'advice' to national leaders in chapters 7—9. Just as in media coverage today, there are also elements of 'personal interest'. The focus here returns to the person of Isaiah once again: the headline might read PROPHET WARNED OF PEER PRESSURE.

Peer pressure

God addresses a 'private' word of warning to the prophet and his band of 'disciples' (vv. 11–16). Just as God challenged Ahaz to be faithful and not to fear the Syro-Ephraimite threat, so with Isaiah. The message to Isaiah is essentially the same: fear God alone! God's prophecy to Isaiah is God's word for Isaiah as well as for the rest of the nation. He is 'not to walk in the way of this people' (v. 11).

These are words of reassurance and encouragement, as well as warning. They represent a confirmation of Isaiah's 'call' in chapter 6, even if no one has acknowledged it since. They affirm once again the alternative reality that he glimpsed: 'But the Lord of hosts, him you shall regard as holy; let him be your fear, and let him be your dread' (v. 13).

At the heart of everything is the overwhelming holiness of the one sovereign God. The truth of that reality does not rest on the rumours and responses of the people of Jerusalem. It does not matter how isolated or misunderstood Isaiah may be (verse 12 suggests that he may have been accused of conspiracy). There is a single truth and to this Isaiah must cling.

God is his refuge and sanctuary, the 'brick' that holds him secure (v. 14). Verses 14 and 15 borrow some classic language from the Psalms. Material that boasts of Zion's glory, that celebrates Jerusalem's destiny, is turned upside down here. This is a typical prophetic inversion: the stone intended to offer a solid foundation becomes a stumbling block. This very image is used again in the New Testament in 1 Peter 2:4–8, where the stone is the living cornerstone, identified with Christ. The image helps to explain the complex intertwining of judgment and hope: it depends on how people respond. For many of the inhabitants of Jerusalem, God has become a stumbling stone, bringing them to fall. For the judgment of God has not resulted in repentance, but hardening and the heightening of evil (8:19—9:1).

Fear

The 'conspiracy theory' of history arises when there is fear. In their suspicion and paranoia, the people resort to occult practices (v. 19) in an effort to reassert control. The tragedy, of course, is that the dubious search for guidance and security amid unknown and devious powers compounds the fear. It also undermines the very guidance and security that has already been offered in God.

Isaiah is called to fear, but not to fear what they fear (v. 12). The reminder of God's terrifying holiness—of the vision that propelled Isaiah to approach Ahaz in the first place—sums up everything from 7:1 onwards. In what, or whom, do we trust? Not to fear God, in the face of calamity, is sheer foolishness in the end, for God is the one fact who cannot ultimately be overlooked (vv. 13–15). Even though to fear God is far from comfortable (it includes dread in verse 13), anything else is insanity.

In verse 17, Isaiah demonstrates the kind of fear to which we are called: 'I will wait for the Lord... I will hope in him'. To be sure, God is hiding his face from the house of Jacob, but Isaiah lives in expectant dependence. God will not hide for ever, but will enact another new thing. Isaiah's ability to wait is aided by the signs and symbols God has given (v. 18). The very existence of his children, as well as the evocative names given to them, was testimony to God's work among his people both in judgment and hope. It is remarkable how Isaiah continually insists fully on both aspects. Because God dwells on Mount Zion (v. 18; as also 2:2), the coming gloom could only be temporary.

God's judgment is not an end in itself, but a means. Isaiah 9:1 declares that it is the means whereby God's goodness can be manifested. This will be manifest in the land around the Sea of Galilee in the north—precisely the area most vulnerable to Assyria, the first part of Israel to be taken over by Tiglath-Pileser around 733BC (2 Kings 15:29).

REFLECTION

Whom do you fear? To what do you cling in the face of pressure, bewilderment or crisis?

BIRTH ANNOUNCEMENT

'A child has been born for us' (v. 6). Here is the standard Hebrew form (found also in Jeremiah 20:15 and Ruth 4:17) to announce the birth of a baby. It is equivalent to the announcement that new parents might submit to a newspaper or send out on a special card. At the same time, the repetition of 'for us' evokes the promise of the name Immanuel, 'God with us', from 7:14. The reference to birth in verse 6 picks up the earlier language—as if this is the concrete fulfilment of the previous prophecy.

This, then, is no ordinary birth. It is the key to the transformation from gloom to glory (9:1). Confirming our earlier suggestion (see pp. 52–53), the birth is a royal birth, most probably that of Hezekiah. As in the language of Psalm 2:7, the birth is associated with his accession as king, a coronation that spells an absolute end to the fated rule of Ahaz and his house. Chapter 7 promised how the throne would be established and upheld in the person of Immanuel. Here in chapter 9 the replacement king is ascribed a number of further titles: 'Wonderful Counsellor, Mighty God, Everlasting Father, Prince of Peace'.

Messianic hope

The work of this king, bringing justice, righteousness and peace, fulfils the vision underlying Isaiah 1—8 as a whole. It is described in the past tense. It thus resembles a song of thanksgiving for what God has already done or, at least, begun to do. Perhaps it looks back during the reign of Hezekiah. The end of verse 7, however, reveals that its complete fulfilment still lies in the future.

This is the sense in which these promises are messianic. In one sense they picture what any king should be, yet they go far beyond what any king ever achieved or even sought. Insofar as they may allude to Hezekiah, their fulfilment was incomplete. This was widely recognized by Jews from the time of the exile onwards.

The language thus came to function as a confession of Israel's belief in a ruler who would replace, once and for all, the unfaithful reign of kings like Ahaz. The basis for conviction lies in the son's name. The significance of a Hebrew name—as, for example, with

Isaiah's two sons (7:3; 8:3)—does not lie in describing the person to whom the name belongs. Rather, the name points to something else, and all these titles point to God: the ruler who will bring justice and peace at last is divine.

From Isaiah to Matthew

It is no small thing for Matthew to quote from Isaiah 9:1–2 in reference to Christ. Matthew 4:14–16 is making the staggering claim that the dazzling light for which Israel had longed over many dark centuries, the one who would truly liberate Israel at last, had come! Yet many did not recognize the Messiah in the person of Jesus. This speaks of the way messianic expectation had come to be dominated more by the means of liberation than by the goal. Jesus was not interested in revolution of the standard military kind; like the titles associated with the Davidic king, he pointed to God.

Matthew's use of Isaiah 9 offers a decisive new application of the prophecy. This does not deny its 'original' reference in promising freedom through Hezekiah from the Ahaz regime, or indeed its relevance subsequently to those in exile who are promised a homecoming. God's promise of freedom and peace—of turning an upside-down world the right way up again—is the outcome of his zeal (v. 7). He will continue to employ human agents to bring about his work of transformation.

REFLECTION

'They rejoice before you as with joy at the harvest, as people exult when dividing plunder…' (v. 3). Does the promise (and, indeed, the gift) of the Messiah excite you this much—with the kind of thrill so intoxicating that it feels almost illicit? God takes pleasure in the delight of those who long, who wait… and who celebrate the end of injustice and oppression (vv. 4–5).

GOD'S OUTSTRETCHED HAND

Can we learn from the mistakes of others? This text appears, originally, to have been a message addressed to Israel in the north (9:8–9). Isaiah reuses it, for (we may presume) it is just as relevant to Judah in the south. Perhaps the prophet invites Judah to consider God's judgment on the northern kingdom in the hope that Judah might review its own response to God. Nathan employed a similar rhetorical technique to bring discernment to King David regarding Bathsheba (2 Samuel 12). If we cannot learn from the mistakes of others, at least we might be better able to identify them.

'For all this...'

These verses are crafted into four sections, separated by a pivotal refrain: 'For all this his anger has not turned away; his hand is stretched out still' (9:12, 17, 21; 10:4). This chorus first appeared at 5:25, concluding the list of woes against Judah. It is as if the poetry here picks up where chapter 5 left off. Indeed, the intervening material (6:1—9:7) conveniently falls into a separate unit, focused on King Ahaz and the Syro-Ephraimite crisis.

God's hand is still stretched out in anger. In the past, God's outstretched arm brought deliverance from Egypt (Exodus 3:20; 6:6). Here the same mighty power is summoned against his people. 'All this' that rouses God's passion concerns the mockery of that very power. By the way they live, the people deny God's sovereignty over all things and his peculiar deliverance of Israel in particular. Are they forgetting that without the God who redeemed them from slavery in Egypt, they would not exist at all? Worse than forgetting: are they self-consciously ignoring the God who sends them a prophet to remind them and warn them?

'Smile—it may never happen'

The problem is not ignorance of God's displeasure; it is outright denial. They are flatly told it will happen, but they still pretend that it won't. The first of the four sections (9:8–11) describes the pride and arrogance that bring people to put confidence in their own prowess. The quotation in verse 10 depicts a people who will not be outdone: their assertiveness makes them blasé, even before the might of God. The second section (9:13–17) pinpoints the leaders—elders, dignitaries, prophets—who are held responsible for leading people astray. In the third section (9:18–21), a picture of a society in mayhem builds up. Corruption seeps all over the land and ruins families and communities. The final outcome, in the fourth section (10:1–4), is a situation of oppression and injustice. The poor, the widows and the orphans—those who have the least—are the first victims, and no one seems to care.

The themes that make up this recital of judgment are becoming familiar. Their order is also significant: from pride, to false leadership, to the breakdown of community, to social injustice. Their recurrence reinforces the tension. The people's mounting denial is matched only by God's mounting anger.

What we end up with is a kind of symbolic liturgy: a series of warnings, each followed by an antiphon like a sting in the tail. It is as if God calls to them, gently at first and then more loudly, until finally he bangs on the door, hoping with each blow to elicit repentance. But they do not answer; indeed, they will not open up. Instead, with each blow, they dig in their heels still further.

REFLECTION

'The people became like fuel for the fire; no one spared another'
(9:19). It is so easy to succumb to the power of our peers, whether
their persuasion or their prowess. Who are 'the Joneses' whom you
seek to keep up with? What fuels your fire (and your folly)? Do
you follow people, or do you follow God?

GOD'S ROD *of* ANGER

The book of Isaiah is getting harder. This chapter seems to offer some varied material relating to an imagined conquest of Judah and Jerusalem by Assyria. In verses 5–11 the focus is on Assyria's macho prowess as it brings rack and ruin. In verses 12–19 God condemns Assyria, despite the fact that it had served as his agent. In verses 20–27 there are words of encouragement to Judah and the repeated promise of a remnant. Finally, verses 28–34 offer an uneasy scenario of God's sovereign work throughout the region.

The mixture of material belies a consistent if chilling theme that is gathering momentum as we travel through these early chapters of Isaiah, concerning God's anger. In the preceding chapters it has been focused against Judah. Here, it unexpectedly turns against Assyria. Even though Assyria is God's instrument—his rod and his staff (v. 5)—that is no guarantee of the nation's safety. As John Goldingay puts it, 'being used by God is never an index of closeness to God (see Matthew 7:22 23)' (p. 79).

Anger and irony

It is easy to conclude that God's anger is insatiable and unpredictable—an all-too-common Old Testament stereotype. This would be inaccurate, however. God's anger at wickedness is a consistent theme throughout both Old and New Testaments. The critique of Assyria makes it clear why God is angry with them. They are proud and self-confident, ascribing no credit to anyone except themselves (vv. 8–9, 12–13). Language normally reserved for God is used for themselves (vv. 13–14), and so they act like God, as if they have control over the destinies of nations.

Here is the irony. God is using a foreign godless agent to bring trouble to his own, also godless, people. It is common for God to employ human agents to carry out his will; indeed, it is characteristic of God's investment in humanity. But this agent is not the normal locus of God's action—an indication of the depth of Judah's problem. And, as it turns out, this is no normal agent: rather than acting *for* God, Assyria acts *as* God.

So we may expect God's anger (if there is justice) to apply to

Assyria as well as to Judah. God appointed Assyria to act as 'rod of my anger' (v. 5). As Proverbs 23:13–14 describes it, the purpose of a rod is to discipline a child so that it may be saved, not to kill it. But Assyria was more than a divine executor: it acted from personal agenda, and the outcome was horrendous atrocity. Thus the crescendo of criticism builds to a fearful 'therefore' in verse 16: punishment for the crimes of war will follow. It comes as a reminder to everyone, no matter how powerful and immune people may seem, that actions have consequences. Again, there is deep irony: symbols of calamity for Judah— motifs of tree and fire, even language about a child (vv. 16–19) —become the symbols of calamity for Assyria.

Remnants

There is a remnant in the case of Assyria (v. 19) as well as in the case of Israel (v. 20). As with the name of Isaiah's son Shear-Jashub ('a remnant shall return', 7:3), the very notion communicates good news and bad news. On the one hand, only a few will survive; on the other hand, at least some will survive.

For Assyria, despite the description 'remnant of trees', there is no hint of regrowth. Indeed, when Assyria was finally cut down in 609BC by the combined forces of Babylon, Media and Persia, nothing ever arose from the stumps again. For the remnant of Israel, however, there is hope beyond this crisis—so long as Israel learns its lesson. Survival is not enough. They must learn to stand firm in faith (7:9)—to lean on God once again, and not on the might of Assyria (v. 20).

History suggests that Israel did not learn its lesson, and so this text has retained its challenge and extended its application to subsequent crises. Thus, in due time, Babylon replaces Assyria as 'rod of God's anger'. Any superpower, even one that serves as an instrument of God, is warned against pride and abuse of power. For it too may fall like a tree (v. 34).

PRAYER

Lord, direct the power of those who govern, that they may use their power humbly and carefully, recognizing that all authority comes from you.

ROOT & BRANCH

If 7:14 hinted at the coming of the Messiah, and 9:1–7 promised it, here in 11:1–9 the reality is most fully expounded. It depicts a glorious era of justice and harmony, which brings together all the distinctive features that have marked Israel's hope in Isaiah so far. First, there is the idea of a felled tree or stump that might be capable of new growth (v. 1; 4:2; 6:11–13). Second, there is the possibility of a successor in the Davidic line who might live up to the calling (vv. 2–5; 7:1–17; 9:1–7). Third, there is the association with a child who somehow encapsulates these hopes (v. 6; 7:14; 9:6).

The picture of growth that springs from a stump demands, first, that the tree be cut down. Accordingly, we may assume that the old house of David is over—Ahaz and his like are gone—exactly as predicted. This cutting off is a prerequisite for what will then develop: a new shoot growing out of the old base, that same unpromising place from which David came—the root of Jesse. This, then, is a thoroughgoing 'root and branch' appraisal of the role, which begins not in a royal palace but with a peasant family.

The spirit of the Lord

This ruler is marked out not by petty pomp (as with the house of David), or by proud power (as with the empire of Assyria), but by the spirit of the Lord that rests on him (v. 2). This is his crucial qualification. The spirit endues wisdom and understanding, counsel and might, knowledge and fear. These qualities are precisely those that were lacking in Judah and Assyria. Assyria, for example, pretended it had wisdom and understanding (10:13); Judah is exiled for want of knowledge (5:13) and, although Judah knew fear, it was misdirected (7:4; 8:12–13; 10:24). These are, rather, attributes of the Mighty God (9:6), which here become real in a human figure as that person lives wholly and fully for God.

Elsewhere in the Old Testament, God's spirit inspires judges, prophets and kings with insight and abilities beyond their normal capacity. This inspiration is often associated with ecstatic experiences and particular tasks: consider Samson (Judges 14:6), Saul (1 Samuel 10:10) and David (1 Samuel 16:13). In each case, evidence of God's spirit is palpable, but its work tends to be spontaneous and short-term rather than predictable and long-term. In this case of the Messiah, the spirit 'rests' on him (v. 2), establishing virtues with which the new ruler is endowed rather than feats he might achieve. Thus the hallmark of his rule is absolute justice. Those who are poor and meek and less visible in society—precisely those who suffered most under the previous regime—are the chief beneficiaries (vv. 3–4). The 'clothing' of righteousness and faithfulness breathes an air of constancy and security (v. 5). This stands in stark contrast to the usual manner in which leaders protect their own position with those who sponsor or elect them—usually the wealthy and powerful—before looking out for the security of others. Here, 'the ruler will be the servant, not because he is too weak to dominate, but because he is strong enough not to need to crush' (Oswalt, p. 278).

The peaceable kingdom

It is the same with the wolf, the leopard and the lion, according to the picture of the new kingdom (vv. 6–9). Here is an extended figure of speech, a glorious picture of the Messiah's reign, where the young and vulnerable—lambs and calves and children—will be at ease with the former symbols of terror and violence. The vision hums with rest and recreation, with joy and trust, with harmony and contentment. In an age of global insecurity, how we long for this! Oh, to live there —or even just a weekend break on God's holy mountain!

But this kingdom is not defined so much geographically as experientially and relationally. The reconciliation experienced through the harmony of 'horizontal' relationships in creation is established through a reconciliation of the fundamental 'vertical' relationship between God and humanity. The new security and trust develop from mutual submission to God, not simply from the mutual (self-interested) agreement of peoples and nations with one another.

Isaiah 2 described the new age in terms of people streaming to the mountain in their longing to know and to live for God better. The kingdom is fulfilled when this knowing is complete: when 'the earth will be full of the knowledge of the Lord as the waters cover the sea' (v. 9).

REFLECTION

Where and how do you long for this kingdom most?

The INTERNATIONAL SIGNAL

On that day, 'when the earth is full of the knowledge of the Lord' (11:9), the shoot that has grown out of Jesse's root will stand as an international signal (v. 10). No brand marketing or world tour is necessary for the Messiah figure of 11:1–9, for the nations will seek him. Their motivation will come from within. Ironically, seeking God is exactly what Judah had failed to do (8:19; 9:13). We are drawn again to the vision of 2:1–4, where the peoples stream to Zion like bees to a honeypot. The attraction is instinctive, magnetic: God's dwelling is glorious. Verse 10 brings together, for the first time, the role of the Messiah with the promises about the future of Zion.

Recovering the remnant

Verse 11 announces that the Lord will extend his hand a second time. The first occasion was at the exodus, when God rescued his people from slavery in Egypt and brought them safely to the promised land. By tradition it was God's outstretched arm that symbolized this act of redemption (Exodus 3:20; 6:6), though earlier in Isaiah the same image of power was inverted to represent the strength of God's anger against those he delivered (5:25; 9:12, 17, 21; 10:4).

The promise that God will extend his hand a second time suggests that he will act to redeem his people again. His action is conceived in similar ways (vv. 15–16), only this time it will be a matter of gathering up all who are scattered and restoring them to their homeland (v. 11). They will be gathered from far-flung places everywhere: the list of places in verse 11 covers the north and south, if not also the east and west, so as to illustrate the four corners of the earth (v. 12). What is more, even the old rivalries between the northern and southern kingdoms, Ephraim (Israel) and Judah, will be ironed out. The 'new' David will bring an era of safety, both internally and externally, reminiscent of that enjoyed under the 'old' David. The kingdom that lies ahead will be one united kingdom: former outcasts and exiles, whether from Ephraim or Judah, will stand together as fellow recipients of God's salvation.

This latter point is striking: for some, it is easier to conceive of a great miracle across the globe—the ingathering and homecoming—

than to contemplate a more local miracle, such as the transformation of tired relationships. But the kingdom demands the resolution of domestic discords as well as the recovery of distant peoples, if the reunion is to be harmonious—if the wolf is to live with the lamb, and the leopard lie down with the kid (v. 6).

'On that day'

This prophecy points to the restoration of Israel 'on that day'. Christians delight in drawing the text to Jesus—as, indeed, did the Gospel writers. Jesus was descended from Jesse (v. 10; compare Matthew 1:6). He came to the lost house of Israel as a shepherd seeking lost sheep (Luke 15:3–7), ministering to the outcasts and exiles (v. 12). And he speaks of the kingdom as an ingathering from north and south and east and west (v. 11; compare Luke 13:29–30). The parallels with Isaiah 11 are hardly coincidental.

This is far from being the only interpretation of the prophecies of Isaiah 11. It may be the most important and final one, but, I suggest, it cannot be our *first* interpretation. These words were understood to find some fulfilment within the experience of ancient Israel, within the horizon of those who received the prophecy of Isaiah. Most immediately, chapter 11 could have been taken to refer to the Israelite homecoming after the Assyrian invasion. More often, it is thought to describe the return from exile after the fall of Judah and Jerusalem to the Babylonians. To some Jews today, it is taken to refer to the recent gathering of Jews in the modern state of Israel.

So, we may ask, on which day is 'that day'? Are there many different ones? There have been several answers to the question of Jewish homecoming, levels of interpretation representing 'layers' of fulfilment that have accumulated over centuries—none of which, tragically, have resulted in decisive restoration. Thus Jesus' contemporaries were among those still waiting for these wonderful promises to be fulfilled when they encountered one who fitted these prophecies as if they were his script. The shoot of Jesse is, finally and most fully, Christ.

REFLECTION

We live between times—between the day of inauguration
and the day of completion of God's kingdom.
How can you hasten its fulfilment?

SONGS *of* PRAISE

One of the purposes of prophecy is to help God's people envisage the future in the way God himself sees it. The previous eleven chapters of Isaiah have created a mosaic that, if we stand back from it, presents a gloomy picture. The future looks dark, because the overarching theme is judgment. God's people have wandered from his ways and his promises. They are urged to turn back, yet it seems too late. They stand condemned. Even though there is a repetition of God's final glorious intentions for the whole of creation, it is hinted that only a remnant of Israel will survive.

Chapter 12 serves as a conclusion to this first section of the book. We might expect it, therefore, to offer a neat summary to drive home once more this depressing message. Instead, it delivers a surprise. These words of rejoicing speak as if God has already accomplished his work of judgment and done glorious things in Zion in the sight of the nations (vv. 1, 4–6).

How do they fit?

These verses are often explained as an editorial addition to First Isaiah, written with the hindsight of return from exile about one hundred years later. This provides a helpful historical frame, a way of understanding the possible origins of such confident praise. Yet we, as those who receive the prophecy of Isaiah in its current form, also need an interpretative frame for understanding these verses in their present context.

I suggest that there are at least two ways to look at them. First, we could read these verses like a script—an advance copy of a special service that, like the judgment and the hope beyond, has already been planned. It is as if God's people are given it to file away until 'that day' (vv. 1, 4) when it will be appropriate for the promised remnant to hold a celebration. As such, these verses confirm the glimmers of hope beyond exile. They confirm that there is something to look forward to. They reinforce the reliability of God's future.

Second, these words of praise could be seen as a worship resource for the present context, despite, or even because of, the predicament of judgment. Perhaps reciting these words might help Judah to turn to God in trust and engage more fully with (rather than denying) all that Isaiah has spoken of in chapters 1—11. Indeed, even a people in crisis must learn to look beyond their immediate context. Here is a form of words with which to acknowledge and refocus on God, an early outworking of Paul's principle to 'give thanks in all circumstances' (1 Thessalonians 5:18).

A new psalm?

Either way, what we have here is a deceptively simple hymn of praise that recalls the past and foreshadows the future. It summarizes the themes of chapters 1—11 while pointing forward to the consolation of Second Isaiah found in chapter 40 onwards.

It is common in scripture to find praise merging with prayer, whereby the experience of the past is brought to bear on situations in the present or future. Many of the Psalms, for example, testify to God's mercies in history so as to build a case for trusting his faithfulness in the future. These verses of Isaiah follow the same pattern; much of the language, as well as the form, is drawn directly from the Psalms. More particularly, the understanding of deliverance is modelled on Israel's definitive event of salvation at the exodus: verse 2 is borrowed from the song of Moses (Exodus 15:2).

These six verses offer Isaiah's theology of salvation in a nutshell. Note how, throughout, the focus is entirely on God. In verse 1, there is testimony to the reality of God's anger, caused by the situation described in chapter 1 but now transformed into comfort and tender forgiveness (to be developed further from chapter 40). In verse 2, God is celebrated for his power to save: contrary to the faithless approach of Ahaz (7:2–9), God is trusted and not feared. The personal testimony of verses 1–2 gives rise to future conviction concerning God's saving work with others (vv. 3–4). The scope of the song expands. As 2:1–4 reminded Israel, their salvation is not an end in itself. Israel is the vehicle by which the nations might also recognize who God is. The God of Israel is the Holy One (v. 6), resonating with Isaiah's overpowering vision of God (6:1–8), and reminding us that God is the only one in whom the power for salvation lies.

REFLECTION

What is your 'song of praise' (whatever your circumstances)?

WORLD JUDGMENT

Isaiah has already touched on international relations, specifically the relationship between Judah and Assyria (chs. 7—11), to assure Judah that even this growing superpower existed under the decisive rule of God. Now the book turns to address the subject of God's governance over every nation. Chapters 13—23 form a unit made up of judgment oracles, addressed to various cities and nations surrounding Judah. These announcements of woe extend to the north, south, east and west, as shown below. God's judgment surrounds Judah—indeed, it includes Judah (22:1–25)—so it may be taken to represent 'everywhere'.

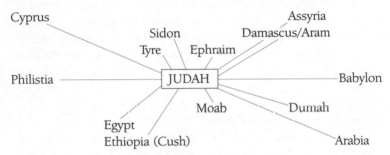

The whole world

Although this whole section of judgment oracles begins with a direct address to Babylon (v. 1), the focus in these first 16 verses is far wider than any one city or nation. An uproar of kingdoms is depicted (v. 4), when the whole earth will be destroyed (v. 5). God will punish the whole world for its evil (v. 11).

This day of God's fierce anger (v. 13) describes the 'day of the Lord' (v. 9), a concept that is already familiar (see chs. 10—11). Thus the international signal of 11:10 is echoed again on a bare hill (v. 2), and the possibility of a remnant (10:20–23) is confirmed even though mortals will be more rare than gold (v. 12). In all other respects, this day is to be feared. The anguish will be like that of a woman in labour: not only in the agony itself, but in other ways too. The pain can be anticipated (v. 6), and it will be sudden (v. 8). Unlike birth, however, the distress continues with tragic and traumatic destruction (v. 16). The language is unrelenting: all that is precious is dashed, plundered and ravished.

The God of love?

This is extreme rhetoric. God's anger is unbridled; his rage is raw. If there were any who counted themselves exempt from the threat of judgment announced earlier in Judah, they can distance themselves no longer. God will punish not only Judah but the world for its evil (v. 11), causing the heavens to tremble and the earth to shake (v. 13). Once the entire creation is destabilized, the one true foundation becomes clear: it is God and God alone.

For some, this depiction will underline a fear and confirm a stereotype commonly associated with the Old Testament: that the God who is sovereign is also a God who is incandescent with rage. On the basis of this chapter, such a conclusion is undeniable. We who inherit the prophecy of Isaiah in an era long after its first delivery must hear again this uncomfortable word of God. God's anger is roused by all pride, arrogance and tyranny (v. 11). His judgment is real, and universal.

At the same time, we must maintain some perspective. God's anger is not the whole story. It is not fundamental to his identity, but a consequence of his holiness. It is God's holiness that is fundamental, and this is the guiding picture of God presented in the book of Isaiah (see ch. 6). Isaiah was privileged and amazed to glimpse the awe-inspiring 'like-nothing-elseness' of God, from which even the seraphs shielded themselves. And this holiness proves contagious: just as, for Isaiah, it became life-changing, so in due time it promises to be world-changing.

In the same way that God's anger brings the heavens to tremble and the earth to shake, so too does God's holiness, when he is worshipped and acknowledged (6:4). Just as the anguish of judgment brings pain like that of a woman in labour, so too, through the groans of labour pain, is it promised that the creation will be liberated from decay and brought into glorious freedom (Romans 8:18–22; compare Isaiah 66:8–9). This declaration of world judgment is not God's only word, or his final word. Yet it is his word.

REFLECTION

The universal scope of God's judgment also speaks of God's universal power: he makes the earth to turn and the moon to shine (v. 10). This is the strongest statement yet that he is in control. Thank him for the assurance here that there is no force greater than God.

CONCERNING BABYLON

It is not insignificant that Babylon is the first of the places to be specifically addressed in these oracles of judgment in chapters 13—23. Even in the eighth century (and even more so in the seventh) it was a showcase of the ancient Near East, a city renowned both culturally and economically. Thus it serves here as 'the glory of kingdoms' (13:19), a model of human achievement and superiority. In due course, it also proves its superiority to the people of Judah, politically and militarily, as the superpower that brings about their exile in 587.

So this indictment of Babylon carries political as well as theological overtones: the nation that will bring down Judah is itself the first that will be brought down by God. With hindsight we can appreciate the heavy irony with which this judgment came to be understood. Just as Isaiah likened Judah to Sodom and Gomorrah at the start (1:9–10), so will Babylon eventually be devastated like those classic cities of sin in Genesis (13:19; see Genesis 18—19).

Humiliation

The oracle takes great pleasure in this announcement. The imagination is kindled to picture wild animals now inhabiting the palaces and squandering their splendour (13:20–22; also 14:23). This furthers the irony, echoing the peaceable kingdom of the messianic age described in 11:6–9. Here also, though, is revolutionary fervour—not so much a tale of 'poacher turned gamekeeper' as the *poached* now being the gamekeepers.

It is just those who had previously been poached—enslaved in Babylon—who are invited to join in a taunt song against the deposed king (14:4–21). His falling has caused not just the slaves but all creation to rise again. The earth receives 'R&R', rest (14:7) and recreation (14:8). Indeed, his falling has also stirred Sheol, the depths, to welcome him into its murky underworld of maggots and worms. There, the king of Babylon joins a museum collection of deposed rulers (14:9). Amid the cruel taunting, a theological explanation is given. Those who set themselves on high are just those who are brought low (14:13–14). Those who made the earth tremble and the kingdoms shake are just those found trembling and shaking themselves (14:16).

Those who showed no mercy to prisoners are just those to whom no mercy is shown (14:17). These people are usurping God, who is the Most High (14:14), the only mover and shaker (6:4; 13:13). It is he alone who shows mercy, who frees prisoners to go home (14:3, 17).

True kingship

In a subtle way, the taunt reminds Judah about the nature of true kingship. These kings of the nations illustrate the problem of all human kingship: the danger of usurping God. This was the reason for God's hesitation in establishing a monarchy in Israel in the first place (see 1 Samuel 8:7), as well as the reason for challenging King Ahaz of Judah earlier in Isaiah (chs. 7—11). Yet the Davidic ideal demonstrates that human kingship under God is possible. The true human king understands his place under God—that his kingship is derived from God's—and thus also his role. This consists in acknowledging God's majesty, demonstrating God's justice and teaching God's law—in short, to rule on behalf of God, to be a channel for the divine.

This taunt may empower Judah to mock some distant puppet-king, but at the same time it functions reflexively. It further underlines the critique of their own king. Ahaz lays claim to the God-given Davidic line, yet in reality he functions more like these kings of the nations. There is a twist in the tail of this taunt, for the king of Judah is fated like these foreigners. His throne turns out to be just as flimsy (14:22; compare 7:9, 17).

Exile and return

Scholars often regard this oracle against Babylon as a late addition to First Isaiah: a taunt that carries the cynicism of oppressed to oppressor, stemming from the slavery of exile. Whether it is a later insertion or whether it simply anticipates ideas that are developed later in Second Isaiah, 14:1–4 introduces some new things: firstly, that Judah will be exiled to an alien land; secondly, that God will re-elect his people; and thirdly, that there will be a triumphant return. With hindsight there can be little doubt that, historically, this text relates Judah's captivity to Babylon's superiority, and subsequently Babylon's fall to Judah's freedom.

PRAYER

Pray that those in leadership might be a channel for the divine.

CONCERNING ASSYRIA & PHILISTIA

After the declaration of God's worldwide judgment on pride (13:1–16) and a sweeping critique of Babylonian-style power (13:17—14:23), the zoom lens narrows and focuses on two particular nations. It is announced that Assyria and Philistia are coming to the end of their respective periods of domination.

Both declarations follow on from chapters 1—12; indeed, chapter 10 has already announced that God's judgment on Assyria would come. These declarations present a continuity and consistency concerning God's work. God's arm, persistently outstretched against Israel (5:25; 9:12, 17, 21; 10:4), is now outstretched over all nations and specifically turned against Assyria (v. 26). Verse 25, 'his yoke shall be removed from them, and his burden from their shoulders', evokes imagery from the royal oracle in 9:1–7, especially 9:4, suggesting the reign of Immanuel. The dating of the oracle against Philistia underlines this expectation: 'in the year that King Ahaz died' (v. 28) mirrors exactly the form in 6:1, 'in the year that King Uzziah died'. There is a vacancy for a new king in Judah, which causes the Davidic hopes and ideals to resurface. Perhaps this time there might be justice and a return to the security the nation once enjoyed.

The predicted fall of Assyria is borne out in history and recounted in chapters 36—37. Assyrian troops were defeated in 701BC, somewhere outside the gates of Jerusalem (37:36). But peace does not follow, because a new threat—Babylon—already looms.

God's plan

This oracle appears to anticipate the theological questions that arise from such disappointment. While predicting the downfall of Assyria, it also affirms the sovereignty of God, as if recognizing that the unfolding of events might cause people to doubt it. The emphasis lies not with any note of victory for Judah, but with God's plan. The Hebrew term is repeated four times in three verses (vv. 24, 26, 27). God 'swears by himself' (v. 24) that he has a plan, and 'so shall it come to pass'.

Despite the vicissitudes of history, God's plan, first raised in chapter 5, is not out of control. In case Israel needs reminding (indeed, as we all need reminding), God is sovereign and his purposes may be trusted. Whatever the changes and chances of this fleeting world, as the ancient prayer puts it, we may rely on God's eternal changelessness. Even if events do not work out as hoped, all is still well from God's vantage point. God's plan does not consist of a detailed predetermining of every detail of history, but an overall persistence of purpose towards which all things are ultimately oriented.

The poor, the needy, the afflicted

The second oracle, against Philistia (vv. 29–31), affirms another vital lesson for Judah. The circumstances for Philistia are far from good, despite the opportunity to rejoice at the death of King Tiglath-Pileser of Assyria, which took place in the mid-720s. An adder is about to appear to replace the snake, and in due course a serpent will come forth from the adder (v. 29). But the emphasis turns to the cause of the most vulnerable in society.

Verse 30 gives an idyllic picture of 'the poor' and 'the needy'. Resonating with the imagery of Psalm 23, they eat and sleep in complete safety. This will be far from the reality for Philistia, just as it was far from the reality in Jerusalem (1:17; 3:14).

So this oracle—ostensibly about Philistia, yet attending to the background function of Zion—reminds God's people about the focus of God's plan. God founded Zion to be a unique haven of rest for the needy among his people (v. 32). This reminder surely sounds a note of reassurance to a people who are themselves feeling needy. Jerusalem was beleaguered by threats from within and without: they were, perhaps, liable to doubt God's plan and forget their calling. But it is also a challenge: will they do the welcoming, will they offer food and rest to those afflicted from Philistia (or Assyria, or Babylon…)? In other words, when it comes to the fulfilment of Zion, are they going to be part of the problem or part of the solution? How and when, then, will the vision of Zion as a place of international refuge and renown (2:2–4) be realized? God's plans are certain, but the details are not predetermined.

PRAYER

Lift to God 'the poor, the needy, the afflicted' who suffer under oppressive regimes today.

CONCERNING MOAB

Like Philistia, Moab is another of Judah's neighbours with whom relations are complicated. They share kinship ties going back to Abraham (Genesis 19:37), but also a history of conflict and hostility (see Numbers 21—25; Judges 3 and 11). Despite the picture of friendship in the book of Ruth, the general background is one of deep hostility between the nations (Zephaniah 2:9).

This oracle consists of a lament concerning Moab. It shares aspects of language and style with Jeremiah 48, even though the order and context are quite different. This suggests that both prophets may have borrowed from a common tradition, a sort of 'stock in trade' of poetry and speech about Moab that was in circulation, distanced from any particular historical situation. The lament responds to an imagined disaster, due to sweep through the cities of Moab from south to north, reducing the whole nation to refugee status. The two main sections of lament (15:1–9 and 16:6–11) are divided by a plea for refuge in Judah (16:1–5) and end by confirming the problem (16:12–14).

Weeping and wailing

In the judgment oracles against Babylon, Assyria and Philistia—especially Babylon—there have been elements of gloating and glee at the news of a foreign nation's downfall. Not so with Moab. Twice in the first verse we hear the cry of horror, 'Moab is undone'. This is the same Hebrew term as in Isaiah's declaration that he personally was 'undone' after seeing God (6:5). Whereas Isaiah cried 'Woe is me' at his undoing, what follows in Moab is a more communal, ritual expression of grief. In each city there is weeping, wailing and melting in tears. Heads are bald, beards are shorn and sackcloth is worn. The loins of Moab quiver; its soul trembles (15:2–4). This oracle is sympathetic; there is no blame.

This appeal for the fugitives is also personal—'my heart cries out for Moab' (15:5)—even though we do not know, as yet, whose is the voice that speaks. In 15:9 comes the shocking surprise: we learn that the voice of compassion belongs to the one who is bringing destruction! God is somehow both crying in pain and also sending further tragedy. This is the logic of Hebrew monotheism: the one God is responsible for it all. There is, apparently, no contradiction.

Steadfast love and faithfulness

The central section of the oracle consists of a petition for asylum in Judah (16:1–5). Moabite society has collapsed, and further destruction is threatened (15:9), but Moab knows what Zion is about. So the Moabites turn to Judah for protection, trusting to find counsel and justice, protection and trust (16:3).

As if acting on the message of the oracle just delivered against Philistia (14:32), the Moabites look to God's provision of safety for the needy among his people in Zion. They seem to be taking Judah's God more seriously than Judah does. What is more, they consider themselves recipients of the promise, counting themselves included among God's people! (As the story of Ruth hints, perhaps Moab might be included in ethnic Israel anyway…)

Here is heavy irony, and a little test for the Judeans. Are they going to be proud and defensive, outraged at the presumption of these 'foreigners', or will they welcome the needy, rejoicing at the prospect of all nations migrating to God's holy mountain (2:2–4)?

The answer to Moab's request (16:3–4a) comes at 16:4b–5. It is a dazzling response concerning future hope, even though it is not clear whether Moab is granted asylum in the present crisis. Theologically, it brings together convictions about Zion and David— that is, about the place where God dwells and the line through which he rules. Relationally, it affirms God's promises to Judah. They are promised exactly what they lack: love and faithfulness, justice and righteousness. Whereas the recent occupants on the throne may have been ineffective, a coming king will fulfil the ideal. Isaiah had trouble getting David's own house to believe this (7:1–17; 9:1–7), but here, prompted (or shamed) by a foreign request, God's messianic promises are repeated.

There is little hint as to when this will happen or who will be involved, only an assurance to needy recipients that justice will come —when God reigns and a son of David reigns. Contemporary historical events and the ultimate day of God's original and final purpose are not disconnected.

REFLECTION

In an age of asylum seekers and refugees, does your attitude
toward them reflect God's priorities?

CONCERNING DAMASCUS, ISRAEL, JUDAH & ALL NATIONS

In this chapter, the oracle begins by addressing Damascus, the capital of Syria (Aram). But it turns out—as indeed with all of these oracles, implicitly or explicitly—to involve a warning to Judah. The passage is complicated, but it is likely that only verses 1–3 relate to Damascus and Aram. The focus moves from Aram to Israel (Ephraim) and then to Judah and Jerusalem (vv. 10–11). At the end, it widens to encompass 'the nations' (vv. 12–14). This works like a film scene, where the camera zooms from one area in the distance to another which is closer, then narrows on to the immediate neighbourhood. Finally it pans back out and across every horizon. From near to far, the scene is devastation.

Like many films, the opening corresponds to certain historical events and circumstances, depicted with poetic licence. The situation for Aram in verses 1–3 is likely to relate to the Syro-Ephraimite war in 734–732BC. The joining of forces between Syria and Ephraim against Assyria, already familiar from chapters 7—12, might explain why the prophecy addresses these two nations together in verse 3. The coalition did indeed prove disastrous: cities were ruined and deserted in both nations. This prophecy predicts the same loss of glory and the same bare remnant for them both. Israelites and foreigners who join together suffer together (as also in 7:7–9).

Trusting God

From verse 4 this situation is addressed within a more theological frame. The nullification of God's beloved people in the northern kingdom of Israel 'on that day' is vividly portrayed. Their glory is brought low, their 'fat' is reduced to 'lean' (v. 4), their harvest is virtually ravaged (vv. 5–6). What is left of the grain and the fruit is a pitiful remnant. Aside from the political realities of Assyria, the reason for this devastation is given in verses 7–8. Israel has been preoccupied with alternatives to God—with its own achievements and with false religious symbols (the altars in verse 8 are probably for Baal). 'On that day', however, people will turn back to God, to the Holy One of Israel.

In verses 10–11 the oracle gets personal. The preceding prophecy about Syria and Ephraim is related to Judah, not to reassure Judah that its enemies will get their come-uppance, but because the Judeans are no better at trusting God. 'For you... have not remembered the Rock' (v. 10). In the Hebrew, 'you' is feminine singular: the one who has forgotten her Saviour is Jerusalem herself.

The language of remembering is reminiscent of Deuteronomy (see, for example, Deuteronomy 8:11–20). In the Hebrew mindset, remembering is a conscious act, a matter for training in order to keep in mind God and his gracious acts. It is not only a mental activity but also a practical one: awareness of God results in living for God. As Jesus put it, those who love God do his will (John 14:15–24).

But Jerusalem—the city where God has lavished his presence and his promises—has forgotten its Maker. This brings its own consequences. Just as with Ephraim, the harvest will be ravaged and its prosperity wasted (vv. 10–11; compare vv. 4–6). The theme is just as in 7:1–9: Judah must trust God and not be afraid of peoples who are rebelling against Assyria and pressing Judah to do so—or their fate will be the same.

A global perspective

Verses 12–14 herald the calamity that is coming to all people everywhere. God is going to put all nations in their place, just as the first of the oracles against the nations made clear (ch. 13). These three verses form the mid-point of this whole section and serve as a reminder of the big picture. Jerusalem faces judgment, but so does everywhere else. On the one hand, we may note that Judah does not receive special treatment from God, given that it has failed to trust. On the other hand, God's judgment of other nations suggests his concern for Jerusalem nevertheless. The nations' judgment relates to their despoiling and plundering of Jerusalem (v. 14), an illustration of God's original promise to Abraham ('I will bless those who bless you, and the one who curses you I will curse', Genesis 12:3a). There is good news as well as bad news for Jerusalem: despite God's judgment, it remains the holy city, the focus of God's plan that 'in you all the families of the earth shall be blessed' (Genesis 12:3b).

REFLECTION

Is your mind trained to remember God and his gracious acts?

CONCERNING ETHIOPIA

This oracle is best read in parallel with Isaiah 2:1–4 concerning the vision for all nations in Jerusalem. The same scenario is envisaged, where 'at that time' all the earth gathers at Mount Zion, 'the place of the name of the Lord of hosts' (v. 7). Whereas Isaiah 2 focused on the end point—what will happen when the nations meet there—the emphasis here concerns the process by which that end point is achieved.

Ambassadors

A land beyond Ethiopia (as if to denote somewhere 'way down south', beyond the known world) is addressed and called to send ambassadors by riverboat with the message from God (vv. 1–2). In modern British idiom, the equivalent might be emissaries from 'Timbuctu'. They are sent to a nation that is unnamed but famed for its power and prowess (v. 2). The lack of label allows the ascription to be attached to any superpower. In the context of the eighth century BC, we might imagine Assyria; in the seventh century, Babylon; in the first century AD, Rome; in the 21st century, perhaps the USA.

These furthest ambassadors summoned to the mightiest people are to raise a signal and blow a trumpet to attract everyone (v. 3). At this point, the oracle turns from the particular (if extreme) to the universal, from the human to the divine, from the historical to the cosmic.

The reign of God

The announcement concerns God's coming reign. After the fanfare to call the nations to attention, the message itself is understated, as if to remind those playing worldly games who is in control. God looks quietly from his dwelling, and bides his time (v. 4).

The subsequent two verses liken this 'time' to the harvest—an association that becomes a regular metaphor in the New Testament (see, for example, Luke 10:2; John 4:35–38; Galatians 6:9; Revelation 14:15). Prior to the harvest of judgment is a time of pruning. Like a vine dresser who prunes the vines, God will trim the shoots that have sprouted (v. 5). They will be left as food for birds and animals (v. 6).

This is sometimes read as the warning of a devastating attack, an ominous confirmation of God's harsh reckoning at the time of judgment. Certainly, it confirms the reality of judgment already stressed in Isaiah. Given that message, though, we might then read these verses more positively, as evidence of God's perfect timing and protection. He acts in the interest of the fruit. He waits until the fruit is formed, not acting too soon or too late. He removes those tendrils and leaves that are not bearing fruit, whatever is unnecessary or an impediment to the crop. This is just the imagery found in Jesus' parable of the weeds (Matthew 13:24–30), as well as in John 15.

The place of the name

Finally, the oracle ends at Mount Zion—the place renowned simply for the name of YHWH—with a glorious ironic twist. The people whom we might most expect to revolt and take destiny into their own hands—in other words, the super-powerful—are just those who come in submission, bearing gifts (v. 7). A rival will pay homage in Jerusalem! Judah may rub its hands with glee at the thought of this reversal, whether thinking of Assyria in the eighth century, or Babylon in the seventh and sixth centuries. But the prophecy of Isaiah is addressed first to Judah, and it suggests that no one can afford to be smug. Rather, they need to be fruitful.

REFLECTION

It is interesting that God doesn't seem to suggest that the mighty power described here will necessarily lose any of its power as a result of undertaking the tasks demanded of it. He only asks for acknowledgment of his supremacy as the Lord.

Does this not give great encouragement to those with burning ambitions to achieve: that God will delight in these achievements, so long as the focus ultimately rests always on him? It's not wrong to succeed where others fail!

SURPRISE... CONCERNING EGYPT

It is possible that this prophecy relates historically to the defeat of Egypt by Assyria under King Sargon in about 720BC. Whether or not this is so, the poetry functions theologically to remind Judah that God is still greater than Pharaoh. Just as he could close Pharaoh's mind at the exodus, so he can bring down the current Egyptian leadership. Therefore, he can formulate strategies for rescuing Judah again, so long as Judah trusts in God and not in Egypt or Egypt's wisdom.

The first 15 verses of the oracle dismantle everything for which Egypt might be envied—first its religious and political stability (vv. 1–4); then its key natural resource, the Nile, and the commerce that depends on it (vv. 5–10); and finally the wisdom for which the country is renowned (vv. 11–15). The critique touches every realm, from religion and politics to geography and economics to philosophy and ideology. There are no grounds left for supposing that Judah might find in Egypt a haven of calm security from the ravages of Assyria.

Temptation

It is remarkable to think that the nation out of which God delivered Israel from oppression might seem to be a tempting ally. The oracle makes this point at its opening, with an imagined glimpse of God riding on a swift cloud to Egypt. This is the exact reverse of the exodus, when God was present in a cloud, leading his people from Egypt to the promised land (Exodus 13:21–22). The parallel continues with a repetition of the natural disasters in the Nile caused previously by the plagues, but this time it is the Egyptians who are subject to a cruel master, rather than the Israelites.

The threat of Assyria in the north grew ever larger for Judah during the eighth century. Increasingly, Judah was tempted to look to Egypt in the south for help. As 20:1 relates—as a warning to Judah—this is what Ashdod (a coastal city in Philistia) had done, to its great detriment. Ashdod was destroyed in 711BC at the hands of the Assyrians, and the inhabitants were carried off. Thus Isaiah's word concerning Egypt is just the same as it had been concerning Assyria: God's people must trust God. Whatever they trust in place of God will prove disastrous.

The great reversal

God's strategy for Judah is unveiled in the prose of the second half of chapter 19. 'In that day' describes not only a day when the Egyptians will tremble at Israel's God, but a day when they will also worship him. God may smite, but he also heals (v. 22), and the latter action far exceeds the former. Suddenly the path of destruction gives way to a staggering restoration: Egypt is included among the people of God.

This vision does not, in fact, come 'suddenly', even though it is unprecedented in extent. In both style and content we may notice how it grows out of preceding material. The series of 'in that day' declarations continues a pattern from 7:18–25, where both Egypt and Assyria were depicted settling together in Israel, amid hostility, scarcity and judgment. The oracle against Egypt (19:1–15) is brought into relation with the oracle against Assyria (14:24–47) by means of the recurring imagery of God's hand and God's plan (14:26; 19:16–17). Furthermore, 'a highway' first described a new exodus journey of the Israelite remnant out of Assyria (11:16). Now the highway is extended, stretching from Egypt to Assyria, and the exodus analogy is applied in reverse. It is the Assyrians and Egyptians who make the journey, and, reconciled, they worship together (19:23). This extraordinary vision is, on the one hand, deeply rooted within the book of Isaiah, and, on the other hand, unimaginable politically and geographically.

The last two verses are breathtaking. God speaks of Egypt and Assyria with the same fondness as he does of Israel—'my people' and 'the work of my hands' (19:25). To think that the language of devotion between God and Israel is explicitly turned to any foreigner... let alone to two long-standing enemies! Even though verse 24 depicts Israel as 'a blessing in the midst of the earth' (the longed-for fulfilment of Isaiah 2:1–5 and, before that, Genesis 12:1–3), Israel is third with Egypt and Assyria. Is this theological promotion for Egypt and Assyria or political promotion for Israel? Either way, Abraham's people remain at the centre of the blessing, though 'ecumenism' is costly. They should prepare to be both generous and flexible!

PRAYER

'Forgive your enemies and bless those who persecute you.'
Lord, help us to be prepared to change our attitudes—locally,
nationally and internationally.

30 ISAIAH 21:1–17

The WILDERNESS *of the* SEA

This chapter has mystified even scholars and commentators. Others tend to skip over it. Yet the issues it raises for interpretation are relevant to all the oracles against the nations (chs. 13—23).

Contemporary or future?

Does this prophecy address contemporary situations, or does it speak to future things well beyond the horizon of Isaiah's day? On the face of it, the oracle seems to be directed to Babylon (vv. 1–10) and, more briefly, to Dumah (an oasis nearby to the west, vv. 11–12) and possibly Arabia (vv. 13–17). (The city of Kedah and the oases of Dedan and Tema are all in north-west Arabia.) But perhaps these place names function symbolically: Dumah means 'silence', for example, and 'Arab' most probably refers to a desert plain. Given that historical references are elusive, it is common to observe apocalyptic overtones in this poetry. Thus the ending of the domination of Babylon —historically, in 539BC by the Persians (Elam and Media united with Persia under Cyrus, v. 2)—now points to something more cosmic. 'The betrayer' and 'the destroyer' might be taken to refer not simply to a historical enemy so much as 'the ultimate enemy'. This apocalyptic dimension is underlined by the fact that the declaration in verse 9, 'Fallen, Fallen is Babylon', is quoted in the book of Revelation (14:8; 18:2), where 'Babylon' functions symbolically.

It seems that the prophecy adopts some of the places and issues of contemporary history, yet speaks through them to situations well beyond the 200-year period covered by the book of Isaiah (from eighth-century Judah to sixth-century exile and return). As with other oracles in Isaiah 13—23, the focus appears to oscillate between the imminent and the ultimate: between the very real material concerns to do with Assyria or Babylon, and the ever-present spiritual concerns about the day of the Lord. Their combination suggests that these two realities are more closely related than we may otherwise think—not just then, but still.

Isaiah's overall agenda

Isaiah's distinctive theme has been the necessity for Judah, and in particular Jerusalem, to trust God. The Judeans need not be afraid of Assyria (or, for that matter, Babylon) or those peoples who are rebelling against Assyria and pressing Judah to do so (see 7:1–9). This theme underlies all the oracles against the nations—Babylon, Assyria, Philistia, Moab, Aram, Ephraim, Ethiopia, Egypt and Tyre—in chapters 13 to 23.

Isaiah has insight into God's priorities and intentions. Even though Assyria and Babylon are proving to be God's means of governing the world in their day, Isaiah knows that God is going to put down these nations and all nations, so it is foolish to put trust in any of them. This oracle asserts once again Isaiah's overriding conviction that the God of Israel is sovereign even in the events of far-off peoples who seem to have little to do with Judah. 'The Lord, the God of Israel, has spoken' (v. 17) and his word happens. Even Balaam (a foreigner) knew, when he uttered God's word concerning Israel, that the blessing or curse would be effective (Numbers 22—24).

What's this got to do with me?

This explains why a Judean prophet speaks of the fate of other peoples. We do not know how many of the foreign nations ever heard God's word concerning them. The word, rather, is addressed to Judah. No analysis is given for God's plan of judgment concerning the other nations—unlike that for Judah. There is no comment about their sins against God or against Judah. It is simply that their majesty and power are a threat to the majesty and power of God. They look and think as if they have taken God's place. Thus, on the one hand, their downfall is a matter of theological necessity; on the other hand, it is a matter for Israel's theological education. The oracles need to shape Judah's worldview and serve as a warning to Judah itself. The point about majesty and power is precisely Isaiah's critique of Judah in 2:6–22. Thus Jerusalem is included among these oracles. Insofar as it operates by the nations' methods, God treats it in the same way as he treats other peoples—as we see in the very next chapter.

REFLECTION

Exactly what this has to do with Judah, it has to do with us. Let's not be taken in by those who seem powerful and impressive, for such splendour cannot last, unless it brings glory to God.

31   ISAIAH 22:1–25

CONCERNING JERUSALEM

This oracle reads just like so many of the others—as a vision of disaster on some foreign people. A people is found rejoicing at a victory, oblivious both to the cost and to the future (vv. 1–3). Only at verse 4 is there an intimation that it concerns God's beloved people, and 'the valley of vision' (v. 5) is to be identified with Jerusalem. The description is surely ironic—for, it turns out, vision is precisely what is lacking.

The poetry presupposes some occasion on which Jerusalem was endangered, attacked and delivered. The event is usually identified with the Assyrian invasion under Sennacherib in 701BC, although Assyria is not explicitly mentioned. The invaders claimed much of Judah but failed to capture Jerusalem (see the account of these events in 2 Kings 18—19), thus explaining the celebration. The absence of a specific reference to Assyria suggests, however, that the particular circumstances are secondary, allowing the text to be reapplied (perhaps in its present form it has been edited) so as to relate also to Judah in the Babylonian period. When Babylon invaded in 593–587BC, 'a battering down of walls' took place (v. 5) and 'the destruction of my beloved people' (v. 4) was complete. This reapplication of the text follows a pattern emerging in chapters 13—23, where there is a consistent attempt to link the Assyrian and Babylonian periods. Both serve to demonstrate the one divine purpose of God for Israel and the nations, described in verses 5–8a as God's 'day'.

The inhabitants of Jerusalem desperately try to prepare an elaborate defence. They address the relevant practical issues, but not the relevant religious issues. They look to their weapons and walls and water, but they do not look to God. Verses 8b–11 are reminiscent of Isaiah's encounter with King Ahaz in 7:1–9. The people seem to fulfil God's original assessment of them precisely: they 'keep listening, but do not comprehend; keep looking, but do not understand' (6:9).

An illegitimate party

God's miraculous deliverance of the city is basically misunderstood by its party-popping inhabitants. Instead of weeping and mourning, Jerusalem's reaction manifests their flagrant disregard of God's will for them (vv. 12–13). Judah learns nothing from the Assyrian threat to its life, from which God has delivered his people. Verse 14 is a pointed way of trying to bring them to their senses: they cannot be forgiven unless they turn.

Whether or not an editorial hand has revised this text in the light of the Babylonian threat, the parallel with subsequent events is striking. In its unfaithful response to the deliverance of 701BC, Israel demonstrated that it was no different from its pagan neighbours: it also failed to reckon with God's plan. This explains why Jerusalem is appropriately addressed in the section of oracles against the nations. It is indistinguishable from all other recalcitrant powers of the Middle East.

Who can be trusted?

Verses 15–25 consist of a rather different prose passage concerning two of King Hezekiah's most important ministers (see 36:3). Essentially, we are given an account of two unjust stewards, as if to issue a warning: 'Never trust a politician!'

We encounter Shebna first, in a graveyard beside the tomb that he is preparing for himself. Even though he seems to be preparing for his death—unlike the people who eat, drink and make merry (v. 13)—he will not have a peaceful burial. He has exploited his authority and appointed himself to a position of honour. As with everyone else, self-interest has blinded him to the gravity of the threat to Jerusalem. Despite his symbols of power and defence, he will be hurled into a foreign land along with the splendid chariots he has commissioned, and will die there.

Shebna is succeeded by Eliakim, who is called God's 'servant' and appears a far more promising candidate. Verses 20–24 lull the reader into a new sense of security concerning the city and line of David. But even the peg that seems secure will give way. Verse 25 points to the collapse of the secure place of Davidic authority. An end to the Davidic dynasty is imminent.

REFLECTION

The two halves of this oracle, read together, suggest that an analogy may be drawn between the public display of unbelief (vv. 1–14) and the private abuse of a divine calling (vv. 15–25). In both cases, the divine grace is betrayed. This calls forth the full intensity of God's judgment. It cannot be escaped, whatever our position. Are we always ready and willing to accept God's judgment?

CONCERNING TYRE

This is the last in the series of oracles against the nations. Looking back, it is hard to say which is the most dramatic. To an eighth-century audience feeling politically threatened, perhaps it would have been the one about the fall of Assyria (14:24–27). To a seventh- or sixth-century audience still feeling vulnerable, no doubt the greatest would have been the picture of the fall of Babylon (13:1—14:23; 21:1–10). To God's people of any period, most incredible is the vision of the highway joining Egypt and Assyria with Israel in worship of God (19:18–25). But to a contemporary 21st-century capitalist economy, undoubtedly the most dramatic oracle is this last one.

Tyre represented a hub for global enterprise in the ancient world. Positioned on the Mediterranean coast (south of modern Beirut), comprising a small island half a mile off the main shore, it formed a natural port (v. 4) and a crossroads for trade and communication from Africa, Europe and Asia. It enjoyed enviable prosperity as well as natural security. Although history suggests that various Assyrian emperors tried to capture it, none succeeded, so it is likely also to have seemed independent and impenetrable.

Thus the shock waves envisaged reverberate all around following the news of Tyre's fall—from Tarshish in Spain and Cyprus in the west to Sidon down the coast and to Egypt further south (vv. 2–5). Tyre's neighbours and trading partners are awed into silence. There is also anguish, for Tyre's downfall will have a knock-on effect on their livelihood. The oracle takes the form of a communal lament culminating in the question, 'How did this all happen?' (v. 8).

God's plan

The prophet answers in a confession, which builds up to the resounding response: 'The Lord of hosts has planned it' (v. 9). He understands that all of this has happened because God has a plan. As asserted repeatedly through this section of oracles concerning the nations, God is demonstrating his sovereign purpose in history. The oracles begin with the whole world in view. The first oracle then focuses on Babylon—the greatest power on land. And here, the last in the series ends with Tyre, addressing the greatest power on the sea.

As Isaiah himself discovered when he encountered God in the temple, the Lord reigns with supreme control over the whole world. Verse 11 emphasizes the point about God's power over sea and over earth's kingdoms, using classic biblical idiom.

God's global plan might, at first, seem a threat to his chosen people. Didn't his plan focus on them? It did, and indeed it does; but not to the exclusion of those beyond Israel, who were always a part of God's plan for universal blessing. So, God's sovereignty over the nations is far from incompatible with his concern for the well-being of Judah. Rather, it may be that God's concern for Judah is a driving force for his action with other nations. Thus, for example, the fall of Babylon permits the prospering of 'Jacob' in its own land (14:1–2). And here in 23:18, the recovery of Tyre will bring extravagant gifts to the people of God.

Tribute to God

It is difficult to discern precisely what historical events the oracle about Tyre refers to, not least because there is no record of a downfall for Tyre. Perhaps the oracle is not meant to be interpreted too literally. It may function, rather, to stretch the imagination to conceive a scenario in which even Tyre—the archetype of prosperity—is humbled. It illustrates a city's 'conversion' to God. The picture of Tyre's recovery after 70 years suggests a thriving economy once again, but this time there is a new and willing orientation to God. It is as if there is now an awareness of God and of God's grace, which brings about a response of generosity to the people of God (vv. 17–18).

The change described in Tyre offers a model of transformation under God. The problem for which each nation has progressively been condemned throughout these oracles is that of autonomy: they have all been playing power games which, ultimately, challenge (rather than acknowledge) the sovereignty of God. Whereas this was true of the 'old Tyre', the new Tyre represents the antidote to the problem. In other respects the city may not have changed much—business and commerce are thriving once again—but this time, Tyre is no longer depicted as acting for itself. Rather, the energy and prosperity of Tyre are channelled to recognize and support the work of God.

PRAYER

Pray that your own city or country be transformed like Tyre.

The BROKEN COVENANT

Chapters 24—27 represent another distinct section of Isaiah. It is sometimes called the 'Isaian apocalypse', given that the visions bear some apocalyptic or eschatological character. That is, they refer to a radically new day, far beyond particular events or nations identified in history. Babylon, for example, is not even mentioned. Rather, the sights are raised to the ultimate purposes of God, consisting of a cosmological judgment of the whole world followed by a final glorious restoration. It is not just a remnant of Israel that is redeemed: the new order involves the salvation of all peoples, when death is banished for ever (25:8).

The section begins by establishing a heavenly perspective. It is as if the Lord holds the fragile planet earth in his hands. It only takes a flick of a finger to disfigure its face or scatter its people (v. 1). Then the global view turns local, as the ripples of God's judgment reach every relationship in every community, cutting across social, economic and political distinctions (v. 2). Nothing is safe or secure: anything and everything will languish and wither (v. 4).

The Lord has spoken this word

The formula 'The Lord has spoken this word' (v. 3) underlines the finality of God's decision while also recalling preceding chapters. Chapter 13 spoke with the same intensity, of God destroying the whole earth (13:5, 9, 11), but there the ultimate end coincided with the fall of Babylon. Here the depiction of 'the end' relates not so much to historical or political concerns, as to a divine decision made on theological grounds. The situation no longer turns on the particular offences of Babylon, but rather on a dimension of evil that causes both heaven and earth to grow sick. The problem is the same as when God sent the flood (Genesis 6:5): the earth has become polluted because God's laws have been ignored and his statutes violated. Chapters 13—23 have exposed the sins of the nations in greater detail. The horrific result is that the everlasting covenant, first made with Noah after the flood, is broken (v. 5).

But isn't the covenant everlasting?

It would seem impossible that an everlasting covenant—if it were genuinely eternal—could be broken. Indeed, when God made this everlasting covenant with every creature on the earth (Genesis 9:9–16), he reassured Noah that 'the waters shall never again become a flood to destroy all flesh'. Despite the fact that, with Noah, God made a new beginning for the world, here with Isaiah he announces the end. This is a tragic pronouncement, a dismantling of God's work of creation all over again. Faithful to his promise, God does not again send a flood. The undoing of creation takes a different form, though the cause and effect are the same. The references to the earth lying polluted (v. 5) and a curse devouring the earth (v. 6) echo precisely the problem at the outset of the flood story (Genesis 6:11). And just as 'on that day all the fountains of the great deep burst forth, and the windows of the heavens were opened' (Genesis 7:11), so here in verse 18 we hear that 'the windows of heaven are opened, and the foundations of the earth tremble'. The result is that the inhabitants of the earth dwindle until few people—as in the days of Noah—are left (v. 6). The effects beyond the human realm are also similar to the flood: all music is stilled, all crops are destroyed and all cities ruined. As verse 11 puts it so vividly, joy reaches its eventide. The sun sets, and misery takes over.

This 'apocalyptic' section of Isaiah, chapters 24—27, is making the point that what seemed unthinkable has, tragically, happened. The everlasting covenant that God established with Noah way back in the mists of time is undone. It is not God who has broken it but the nations, by their assaults of pride and power over centuries, described in the previous section (chs. 13—23). They have returned to the violent ways of their primeval forebears. All notions of human progress must be abandoned!

REFLECTION

How does it feel to be disciplined in this way? When a child is deprived of a toy, or a teenager is deprived of freedom—owing to its abuse—repentance usually follows. But are we ever willing to admit we are wrong? It doesn't get any easier from childhood to adulthood, but it is just as necessary.

34

PRAISING *or* PINING?

When it is known that God is to act decisively in judgment, what is the appropriate response? Verses 14–16 illustrate two very different reactions. Verses 14–16a describe a people who rejoice: these people sing for joy over the majesty of God. The language of giving glory to the God of Israel—which follows conventional patterns of Israelite praise—suggests that the (unnamed) people envisaged here is Israel.

On the other hand, the prophet himself is in torment. Verse 16b demonstrates his personal reaction to the vision of 24:1–13. The prophet's anguish stems from the coming judgment that will overwhelm the entire world, and he is horrified by the 'treachery' that will bring it about (compare 21:2–3). Such a sense of pain, suffered on behalf of others, is typical of a prophet. As we saw earlier, especially in chapter 6, Isaiah engages fully with God's perspective when it might otherwise be attractive to seek escape.

The problem with the Israelite response is not their praise so much as their timing. The language parallels the passages of praise found in Isaiah 12:3–6 and 42:10–12, where a 'new song' is sung in preparation for the entrance of God's new order. But the vision in chapter 24 has depicted the moment of God's apocalyptic judgment on the world, not the implementation of God's rule at Zion. The old order, including the hosts of heaven and the kings of the earth (v. 21), needs to be brought to an end before the new order may be inaugurated. So there is no hope of escape, and certainly no grounds for gloating. It seems that, whether in error or denial, Israel has misread the sign of the times. The vision announces that the longed-for fall of the enemy will coincide with a universal apocalyptic judgment, when Israel will also face judgment. The most appropriate response, therefore, for all people is to 'pine away', beginning—as the prophet himself did—with 'Woe is me!' (v. 16; compare 6:5).

The end of the earth

What follows emphasizes the magnitude of the approaching judgment, extending the litany of destruction that began in 24:1–3. Verse 17 presents scenes of horror poetically ('terror', 'pit' and 'snare' all begin with 'p' in the Hebrew) that are clearly addressed to every 'inhabitant of the earth'. Verse 18 warns that escaping one danger only leads to a worse fate—a prophetic technique to emphasize the all-encompassing catastrophe. The imagery is developed above as well as below the earth, echoing the flood narrative concerning the 'windows of heaven' (Genesis 7:11). Meanwhile, the earth itself, which normally provides a firm foundation for life, is diminished in stature and security to the point of ridicule. It wobbles helplessly, staggering like a drunkard out of control until it drops in a heavy heap, unable to recover (vv. 19–20). This cosmic shake-up is completed in conventional 'Armageddon' terms with the darkening of the sun and moon (v. 23).

The Lord will reign

The universal judgment continues to be depicted as an extension of that which has already been conceived with respect to Babylon. Just as the mighty king of Babylon was taunted with the prospect of being lowered to a pit (14:15–21), so now he is joined by the host of heaven as well as other earthly kings (v. 22). At the same time, this scene of destruction expands the announcement of universal punishment with which God commissioned Isaiah near the beginning of the book. Chapter 6 spoke of a destruction touching all humanity and every nation on earth, until 'vast is the emptiness in the midst of the land' (6:12). It also announced that there would be a tenth that remained, to be burned again, that a holy seed might emerge. This may explain the few who are left (v. 6), or the voices that praise (v. 16), or the elders who glimpse God's glory (v. 23); for the goal of God's judgment is here made absolutely clear: 'the Lord of hosts will reign on Mount Zion and in Jerusalem'. Exactly what Isaiah himself experienced on a personal level in chapter 6 is what the new order promises on a corporate level to those who remain faithful. It is a faithfulness that begins with 'Woe is me!'

PRAYER

Echo Isaiah's cry, 'Woe is me!' beginning with yourself, extending to your community and reaching to the ends of the earth.

A MODEL *for* PRAISE

Following on from the challenge concerning praise in the last section, this chapter offers a definitive presentation of praise. The praise is a response first to God's decisive intervention of world judgment (vv. 2–5) and second to the promise of God's salvation for Israel and the nations (vv. 6–10a). The chapter ends on a more salutary note, with the recognition that there remain pockets of resistance (in this case, Moab) to God's purposes. Because of its continuing pride, Moab falls outside the arena of God's salvation.

These verses of praise follow the conventional pattern of a thanksgiving psalm. From the start, God's lordship is acknowledged, displacing any sense of one's own autonomy and affirming life as a response to this most fundamental relationship. 'O Lord, you are my God' functions like a simple creed, a confession of faith.

The reasons for praise are spelt out in general terms in verse 1, and in more specific aspects (seemingly both positive and negative) in verses 2–3 and 4–5. We are not told which fortified city is a ruin: as in 24:10, the city fulfils a representative function (it may be any city), although there is background resonance with Babylon as a 'palace of aliens' that 'will never be rebuilt' (compare 13:20; 14:22). Judgment is good news for those with nothing to lose, since God acts for the vulnerable and against the powerful. But here, those who rejoice include the strong and the ruthless (v. 3) even though they are disarmed (v. 5). They rejoice because of what God has done for the poor and the needy (vv. 3–4). The fact that God offers this group 'a shelter from the rainstorm and a shade from the heat' echoes the dream for a canopy over Mount Zion expressed earlier in 4:5–6.

The new order

Although the shelter is not identified with Zion in verse 4, the next section of praise in verses 6–9 makes the allusion even more specific. Following the ruin of worldwide judgment, and the end of the old order of the ruthless and the alien, the new order is inaugurated with God's reign on Mount Zion. As 24:23 promised, God's glory is revealed. This includes participation in a sumptuous feast (v. 6), the abolition of death (v. 7), the end of pain and disgrace (v. 8) and the reassurance of salvation (v. 9).

Most significant of all, it is emphasized that the new order of divine rule includes all peoples at the festal meal. The banquet is not just for 'elders' (24:23)—which might be taken to refer to those Israelites privileged to accompany Moses when he shared a meal with God at Sinai (compare Exodus 24:9–11). Here, the inclusion of 'all peoples... all nations... all faces...' is stressed repeatedly in verses 6, 7 and 8. This extends the international ideal of 2:2–4, where the nations stream to the mountain to learn of God's ways. It also generalizes the promise of 19:18–25 that identified particular nations (Egypt and Assyria) turning to God in blessing.

The new order is a theme that grows in strength throughout both Second and Third Isaiah, to the final two chapters where the new heaven and new earth are most fully developed (65:17–25; 66:22–23). This language and imagery re-emerge in the book of Revelation.

Beyond self-interest

This psalm of praise seems to fit a 'gap'. It is as if it belongs in the gap between orders—that is, after the desolation of God's judgment on the old order and before the inauguration of his reign in the new. Here is faithful Israel, presented as waiting upon God (a favourite motif in the psalter: see, for example, Psalm 25:3, 5, 21). There is a prayerful attitude of eager expectancy—a patient conviction that light will follow darkness, that joy will come even if God is currently hiding his face. This is fuelled by the anticipated celebration when salvation finally comes (v. 9).

It is not only Israel's patient obedience that marks this out as a paradigm of prayer. It is also the maturity of perspective—a concern for the poor, a welcome to all nations—that breathes an open, non-defensive engagement with the agenda that God has unveiled through Isaiah so far. There is no tension and no fear here between the national and the universal: all have been judged, and all may be saved, even though (as Moab demonstrates) some may exercise their God-given freedom to reject his gracious invitation. There is cause for whole-hearted celebration on the holy hill of Zion, for God's salvation is available to all.

THINK

How often do we praise God as in the wonderful prayer of verse 1?

WAITING & TRUSTING

The tone of this chapter is quite different from the last. Although it notes the joy in God's victory over oppression (v. 1, 19), there is no hint of celebration. The praise and prayer seem to concern a faithful yet flagging group of survivors. They are seeking to trust God, but are struggling in the 'gap' between judgment and restoration. It is common to relate this passage to the Israelites in the period of exile around the time of Babylon's fall, although there are no specific historical references. It might involve the (eighth-century) prophet Isaiah envisaging the future (sixth-century) scenario, or it could have arisen much later from the survivors' situation and have then been incorporated into the first part of Isaiah. Neither option matters significantly for our contemporary appropriation of the text. Given the absence of a specific context, it may be applied to any group of God's faithful people between the times, struggling amid the death throes of an old order and awaiting the fullness of the next.

Present versus future realities

The vision of God's universal judgment and salvation (chs. 24—25) is the backdrop. God will bring an end to the present world arrangements: this conviction prompts the 'hymn' of verses 1–6. Picture the new Jerusalem 'on that day'. The walls will be rebuilt, making it strong (v. 1), yet the gates will be kept open for the gathering of the righteous from all nations (v. 2). There will be no need to be defensive: such openness is possible given the peace that stems from trusting God rather than one's own security. Where verse 3 offers reassurance— 'peace' occurs twice, suggesting 'perfect peace' or 'double well-being' —verse 4 follows with an exhortation to trust. 'Trust' becomes an imperative. It is not just a recommendation: it is vital for the faithful to be faithful. Verses 5–6 also serve to prevent any easy triumphalism. It is the poor and needy who will triumph, not those who find comfort, security or pride in the present.

What follows in verses 7–21 is a lament, a communally voiced complaint stemming from the experience of the distance between present circumstance and future promise. The faithful who testify to God's victory also know the pain of divine and human judgment.

They are, indeed, 'the poor and needy'. As onlookers we might commend their honesty: here is no bland ('I'm fine') denial of problems, but a free and frank expression of all that is unresolved. If God is sovereign, then it follows that such complaints should be voiced to him in prayer, rather than ignored or 'gossiped' among fellow Israelites.

Dogged determination

The same group who sing of God's victory and urge one another to trust are also depicted expressing just how hard it is to maintain that trust. If trust is 'continuing to rely with dogged determination without respect to circumstance' (Walter Brueggemann) then their doggedness is wearing thin. The community of Israel after the exile was small, overwhelmed by the tasks of rebuilding and with many reasons to give up on God. Yet their lament also expresses confidence—a simple conviction that God attends to the path of the righteous (v. 7). Obedience is the grounds for hope.

So in prayer they yearn for God to make his name known in the world (vv. 8–9), especially with regard to the wicked (vv. 10–11). At the same time they affirm their faith in God alone, recognizing all that he has done for them in the past (vv. 12–15) even while acknowledging their disappointment (vv. 16–18). It is a moving prayer. The pain is expressed in such vivid terms that those who know the agony of childbirth will find themselves writhing again—only to find that the labour is in vain (vv. 17–18). The expression of thirsting for God is equally stirring (vv. 8–9a), perhaps a longing that only those who have trusted God through hard times can fully relate to. Together, these expressions form a potent plea for mercy as well as an uncompromising rejection of complacency.

The last three verses present a staggering response to the cries of those living between promise and fulfilment. Verse 19 offers the first statement in the Old Testament about resurrection: a divine reassurance that salvation belongs to a bigger story than the present age, reaching beyond the grave to a final victory over death itself. This is a confession to sustain the faithful, whatever the pain and misery of the present age, for God will come to execute justice in the world (v. 21). Indeed, Christians now confess that God has come—in Christ.

REFLECTION

Who said faith was easy? Let verse 4 inspire you to doggedness.

A NEW SONG *of the* VINEYARD

This chapter completes the section named the apocalypse of Isaiah (chs. 24—27). In keeping with the nature of apocalyptic, there are no historical markers: the text transcends any single historical moment in Israel's experience. It relates to any who find themselves at the juncture between judgment and salvation, to instruct them in faithful living.

The community that rejoices in God's salvation in 25:6 finds itself yearning for some encouragement in chapter 26. Chapter 27 provides a fitting conclusion, summarizing God's purposes with a renewed pledge of his commitment and his victory, expressed in four aspects.

First, verse 1 describes God's cosmological victory over evil in the new age. Leviathan is a mythological creature representing the forces of chaos that threaten the safety and coherence of creation. These forces are embodied throughout much ancient Near Eastern literature in the form of a sea monster—just as, later in Jewish thought, they come to be focused on the figure of Satan. This creature is depicted on the loose, seeking to undermine God's metaphysical and moral order. The death of Leviathan announces God's final conquest over the source of evil and thus the end of helpless fear among his people.

A love song, again

Secondly, the heart of the chapter consists of a renewed vision for Israel as God's vineyard: God's chosen, treasured possession. To appreciate fully the new song of the vineyard in verses 2–6, it is worth re-reading the earlier song of the vineyard in 5:1–7, since the new song represents an allegory that redevelops each aspect of the old. Whereas previously the garden was being abandoned, now God is its keeper (v. 3). Whereas previously it was dying from drought, now God himself waters it constantly (v. 3). Whereas previously thorns and briers grew to choke the neglected fruit that roused God's anger, now God intervenes to root out these enemies, in order to protect his vineyard (v. 4). Whereas previously its fate was due to punishment by God, now God has no further wrath. Whereas previously there was bloodshed in place of justice, and oppression in place of righteousness, now it is the setting for God's peace (v. 5; compare 26:3).

Whereas previously the vineyard yielded a pitiful harvest—until it became a wasteland—now it produces so much fruit that it will fill the whole world (v. 6).

The transformation symbolizes the divine reversal: the new era in which Israel is no longer the victim of God's wrath, but the recipient of his lavish devotion. A love song that had previously turned sour is revisited; Israel hears it once again, sung with renewed passion. The reader can almost hear the new green buds of Israel's joy bursting in time to the music. Israel will thrive once again, suffering and scarcity will turn to blossom and plenty, and these blessings will reach the ends of the earth.

The third section of this conclusion (vv. 7–11) steps behind the joyful reversal to address Israel's guilt. The Hebrew is difficult, and precise interpretation much disputed. Verse 7 seems to open up the question of the difference between God's handling of his people and of the nations. In response, verse 9 affirms that Israel has been appropriately punished, given their unfaithfulness to God, particularly in regard to false worship. Their full restoration, however, depends upon future obedience. This contrasts with the response of other nations to God's judgment—notably 'the fortified city' (v. 10), symbolizing those who continue to stand for earthly power and oppression. Despite having experienced the wrath of God, they have not learnt. God's punishment was disciplinary, but redemption is not available to those who reject God's sovereignty.

The harvest

The fourth and final anticipation concerning 'that day' consists of an assurance that there will be—in God's time, signalled by a trumpet call—a regrouping of Israel at the place of true worship, the holy mountain in Jerusalem. The goal of God's purposes remains the centripetal gathering of his people at Zion, those lost and scattered from the north (Euphrates) to the south (Egypt). The image of threshing introduces a note of warning, as also found in the Gospels (see Matthew 3:12; 13:30): the work of the harvester involves separating the grain from the chaff.

REFLECTION

How might God's love song to you go?
Like chapter 5, or chapter 27?

A Precious Cornerstone

Chapters 28—33 return to the same style of preaching as chapters 1—12. They have the feel of a 'sequel' sermon series, following similar themes. There are six oracles of woe, perhaps echoing the six 'woes' of chapter 5; but they address a subsequent period, perhaps 705–701BC. King Ahaz is replaced by King Hezekiah in Judah, and the hoped-for alliance with Assyria transfers to a hoped-for alliance with Egypt—since Assyria has become the big threat.

Plus ça change!

Following a major section concerning the nations (both chs. 13—23 and 24—27), we might hope that God's people would have learned a lesson. Yet, in these next oracles, they are no more likely to trust God and no less likely to trust in military might or foreign allies. Alas, it seems that nothing has changed. But God, in patient generosity, offers yet another explanation of judgment and yet another opportunity for faith and salvation.

The opening expression of judgment in the first of these six oracles is focused on Ephraim (the northern kingdom, vv. 1–6), a nation whose beauty has been bloated by indulgence. Although there is reassurance concerning an eventual remnant 'on that day' (vv. 5–6), the nation's fall is presented as inevitable.

Drunken leadership

The reference to Ephraim seems to function as a prophetic technique —a flashback reminder—to startle Judah concerning its fate, for the fall of Samaria to Assyria in 721BC led ultimately to the Assyrian attack on Jerusalem in 701BC. The second part of the oracle stresses the analogy between Ephraim and Judah: just as drunken revelry led to the fate of the northern kingdom, so it will bring down the southern kingdom also (vv. 7–13).

The big problem in Judah lies with the priests and prophets: instead of being filled with the Spirit, they are filled with wine (compare Ephesians 5:18). They encounter Isaiah in a scene of inebriated debauchery and taunt him, complaining that he has treated them like children and spoken to them in gibberish (vv. 7–10). The response they receive is loaded with irony: as they spoke of Isaiah, so (through Isaiah) God speaks to them. As they judge, so they are judged. For those who refuse to comprehend the word of God, it becomes incomprehensible. Worse, indeed—for this group who presume to discern the things of God, God's word becomes a snare (v. 13; compare 8:15).

False refuge; true refuge

This is explained further in the third section of the oracle (vv. 14–22). God's sentence of judgment is spelled out to scoffers who rule in Jerusalem. An overwhelming scourge will expose the lies and false refuge of prophets and priests. They will be swept away by means of hailstorm and flood, just as it happened to Ephraim (vv. 2, 15, 17). Beware those who hide behind a godly job title without faithfully fulfilling the role! But this is not like Noah's flood: for those who trust, whose lives are marked by justice and righteousness rather than lies and falsehood, there will be an immovable island of safety. For God is laying a foundation stone, a precious cornerstone, in Zion (v. 16).

The image of God as a stone or rock—already familiar in Isaiah (8:14–15; 17:10)—is double-edged. The same stone may cause some to stumble while providing others with safety and sanctuary. The positive aspect stressed in verses 16–17a appears (from textual evidence) to be an insertion. In the final form of the oracle as we receive it, this serves to underline the element of human choice. Whether God is perceived as punisher or protector depends upon the human response of faith. God is in the process of laying a new foundation stone, which is more than founding the temple or securing the Davidic dynasty. It is a haven amid the storm of judgment ahead, for those who look to God in trust and faith. This suggests that the promised remnant is not a future miracle but a present reality even during the period of Israel's judgment: God's new creation is emerging already, through faith.

The last section of the oracle (vv. 23–29) reads like a passage from Proverbs. By observing the shrewd work of a farmer, we may understand that the ways of God are wise and deliberate. Just as it seems strange and alien to tear open the ground before sowing the seed, so apparently violent acts of judgment follow God's purpose.

REFLECTION

Patience, generosity, wisdom, humour—are you familiar with these divine hallmarks?

IN *an* INSTANT

This chapter, complicated though it seems, continues the theme of the inability of Judah to comprehend God's strange plan. This strangeness is highlighted in verses 1–8, where God seems to both attack and defend Jerusalem ('Ariel' refers to Jerusalem). Verse 1 begins with 'Woe to Ariel', yet at verse 5 God's encampment against Ariel seems suddenly to turn 'in an instant' so as to protect Ariel from the hostile nations who fight against her.

Some have interpreted this as an oracle of judgment, followed by an oracle of salvation; a pessimistic prophecy tailed (and, by implication, revised) by an optimistic one. The first oracle is thought typical of Isaiah's critique of Zion and Jerusalem (as found especially in chs. 1—12), while the second is alleged to stem from a subsequent addition, following the extraordinary deliverance of Jerusalem from Assyria in 701BC (see 37:36–7). But God's judgment of Zion is not incompatible with his judgment on those nations who threaten Zion. Both Judah and the nations are subject to God's final sovereignty. Thus the movement from verses 1–4 to 5–8 does not necessarily presume that the judgment against Zion is suddenly lifted. Rather, the judgment levelled at Zion also applies to the nations when they stand against the one who is Lord of all nations. As it now stands, therefore, verses 1–8 illustrate the strangeness of the purpose of God, who both attacks and defends Jerusalem. Indeed, he attacks Jerusalem by means of nations, Assyria and Babylon, whom he in turn condemns. This is underlined by the military language of God's assault on Jerusalem—encamp, besiege, attack towers, siege-works (v. 3)—which mirrors techniques associated with the Assyrian army.

Stupidity and amazement

The next section, verses 9–14, develops the theme of the stupidity of those in Jerusalem who are unable to understand what is going on. This was sounded at the very outset of Isaiah (1:2–3), and the notions of Israel's increasing blindness and deafness were addressed in Isaiah's vision and call (6:9–10). Here is an example of Israel's hardening: their senseless stupor is the consequence of their rejection of God's will. This, in turn, prevents them from comprehending

God's words further. Superficial acts of worship (v. 13) are a further corollary of this situation of hardening. Judah is only going through the motions, and is failing the perennial challenge of connecting worship to life.

Nevertheless, in his strange purposes God responds with a promise to perform further miracles, again. The same word for doing something 'amazing, wonderful, marvellous' is repeated three times in verse 14. 'Again' underlines that God has done this in the past, most of all in the deliverance of Israel from Egypt at the exodus. Perhaps those in a stupor even have to be reminded of this event. These wonders will demonstrate real wisdom; they may also provide the cure for empty worship.

Good news or bad news?

Despite the fact that God's plans are too deep for many to comprehend, there exist those who consider their own plans too deep for God (v. 15). Those who attempt such arrogant autonomy are described vividly as clay that tries to speak to its potter, or as a creature that tries to deny or undermine its creator (v. 16).

For the third time in this chapter there is an announcement of imminent rehabilitation (vv. 5, 14, 18). The Potter, the Creator—the one so misunderstood by those who discount the divine and struggle with their own petty preoccupations—is about to demonstrate his true power. He will turn society upside down. Presumably the creature and the clay will be confused by this work of transformation, but they will not be able to deny it. How we react depends on who we are. Those with little or nothing gain everything (vv. 18–19), while those who have most to lose come out with nothing (vv. 20–21). The deaf hear; the blind see; the meek and the needy rejoice. This is the precise reversal of the situation described in verses 9–12 (and 6:9–10). Meanwhile, both tyrants (the term used of ruthless outsiders, v. 5) and scoffers (the term used of mocking insiders, 28:14, 22) are brought together in verse 20; we may have thought these two belonged in different categories, but it turns out that they share the same fate.

PRAYER

Lord, I am clay in your hands: form me as you will.

Rebellious Children

This section of Isaiah (chs. 28—33) builds a growing sense of history repeating itself, as God's people hear of their impending doom and of their urgent need to trust God again. Just as in the time of Ahaz seeking alliance with Assyria, they are again addressed as 'rebellious children... rebellious people, faithless children' (vv. 1, 9; compare 1:2, 5, 28). Now, under Hezekiah, they are seeking alliance with Egypt because Assyria has become the aggressor. This first half of chapter 30 concerns Judah's proper stance towards Egypt.

The prophet is consistent, repeating the same old concern to trust, but in new ways for this new situation. It is the task of any faithful preacher to remind people of what they (should) already know, but in new words, so that they might hear afresh. If these Israelites could embrace the tradition in which they sit, then they could relate again to the God who is bigger than their current circumstances. Alas, it turns out that they are a people who cannot help themselves (vv. 6–7).

Defiance and alliance

The chapter begins with a reminder of God's plan. It is the big picture, not the present circumstances, that enables trust. As wayward, wilful children, they not only ignore the plan but defy God in seeking alliance with Egypt (v. 1). It is not necessarily wrong to seek help from another nation. As we shall see further on in Isaiah, Israel in exile receives help from Persia, God's chosen instrument of rescue. The problem here is that they are obstinately doing exactly what God told them not to do—for the second time! Furthermore, they seek from Egypt 'refuge... protection... shelter' (v. 2), which are just the metaphors that describe what God alone offers (see Psalm 91:1; 121:5). This is tantamount to blasphemy.

Verses 3–4 hint at the hopes for enhancing Judah's international standing under Pharaoh (Zoan and Hanes stand for the whole of Egypt, lying respectively in the far north and far south). What foolish naïvety, given Egypt's record of hostility toward Israel and Israel's God! Indeed, this alliance 'brings neither help nor profit, only shame and disgrace' (v. 5, compare vv. 3, 7). The same language is used elsewhere in Isaiah of the pointless pursuit of other gods (44:9–10), thus underlining the real problem. God's people are turning away from their God. Verse 6 goes further, hinting colourfully at a dangerous backtracking of Israel's definitive exodus journey. These people are unravelling their own story of salvation, just when Rahab—mythical symbol of Egypt's power—is paralysed (v. 7)!

Smooth things... and broken things

Logic might suggest that if they abandoned God, God would abandon them. Indeed, they want to cease to be his people (v. 11). Whereas the last chapter proclaimed that day on which the deaf will hear and the blind will see (29:18), here we discover people intentionally choosing to be both deaf and blind. Whereas the word of God is freely available (in oral and written forms, from prophets and seers), these people perversely ignore what is right. They opt instead for the ego-massage of 'smooth things' and the fantasy world of illusion (vv. 8–10). But God does not abandon his people so easily, even the rebellious and faithless who ask for it. Rather, he demonstrates his grace yet again.

He responds with vivid imagery, the kind of language that these 'children'—even toddlers in their 'terrible twos'—might understand. The message could be compared to the tale of Humpty Dumpty. The accumulation of defiance and deceit is such that there will be a 'great fall'—as if the wall cannot bear the burden of oppression and deceit (v. 13). The crash will be catastrophic and instantaneous, so serious that the Potter's vessels will be impossible to mend, in human terms. Thus God urges his people to return and rest, to trust in him rather than in cavalry (vv. 15–16). (Only later is God's passion for mending broken things revealed.)

Judah, however, chooses feverish activity, not rest; and places its security in military might, not in God. The cost will be a different sort of rest: a bare flagpole—no longer even a shelter—stranded on a lonely hillside. The signal is silence, desolation (v. 17; compare 1:8; 5:26). As the seers of Ecclesiastes describe it, the opposite of rest is a chasing after wind (Ecclesiastes 4:6): utter foolishness.

PRAYER

Lord, give me ears to hear you and eyes to see you.

THIS IS *the* WAY; WALK *in* IT

The idea of a naked flagpole flapping helplessly in the wind is a tragic and humiliating prospect for a people charged with holding up God's banner to summon the distant nations of the world (v. 17; 5:26). It is another reminder, and a painful one, of God's commitment to his plan. Whatever the cooperation of his people, God's purposes will prevail. Who can possibly understand how they will prevail? If God operated with a blueprint, then it must have been revised a thousand times! Not only do God's intentions prevail, but so does his commitment to fulfil them through his people, despite their stubbornness. Isaiah 30:15–16 described them refusing God's offer to return and trust, just as Ahaz refused God's offer of a sign a generation earlier (7:10–12). God's intention to be gracious still prevails: he mends the unmendable; he re-forms the vessels that were smashed to smithereens.

Waiting

Immediately following the declarations of warning and woe, verse 18 begins, 'Therefore the Lord waits to be gracious...' We are invited to follow the logic: just as God continues to commit to his plan, so God waits in commitment to his people, even if they run off elsewhere. He will not give up. It is a picture of the loving parent who keeps the front door open, ever hopeful that the rebellious teenager will return; of the prodigal's father, arms outstretched in eagerness and excitement, waiting to embrace his bedraggled child (Luke 15). God waits to be gracious, and he waits for his people to reciprocate: 'Blessed are all those who wait for him'.

The situation of rebellion and judgment is put into perspective here (vv. 18–21). On the one hand, the Lord brings 'the bread of adversity and the water of affliction': he is, indeed, responsible for such trials, when he may hide himself. Nevertheless, God hears the cry of his people, just as he heard the cry of the Israelites in Egypt (Exodus 2:23–24), and he responds. It is as if the healthy human life under God involves a pattern of crying to him and receiving from him. Then the people have eyes that see and ears that hear again (compare 30:9–10). They see their 'Teacher' and they hear his teaching: 'This is the way; walk in it.'

This message is far from new: it sums up the nature and purpose of God's law, which was given as a guide for living within the privileged covenant relationship, a way of enjoying life at its best (see Exodus 19:5–6). Yet it came to be seen as a burden rather than a gift, a symbol of constraint rather than honour. Here, verse 21 anticipates a time when the guidance is received warmly once again, and the sentiment echoes Psalm 119: 'Delight in the law of the Lord'.

A second chance

The consequences are multi-faceted and technicoloured (vv. 22–26). Idols—a contributing factor to the conditions of adversity (8:19–22)—are defiled and scattered, this time in repentance. It rains again (the reversal of the curse of 5:6) and so agriculture flourishes: the crops grow rich and plentiful; the livestock share the harvest. We may recall here the peaceable animal kingdom of 11:6–9, and join in feasting and dancing with bears! Nature is transformed—brooks flow with water; moon and sun shine brightly—representing the transformation of human life also. Above all, wounds are healed.

The context invites us to see those wounds as the self-inflicted consequences for a people determined to ignore and defy God. Owing to wilful disobedience, they experienced the negative side of God's justice: punishment and withdrawal. Despite their best attempts at self-harm, this rebellion does not determine their final end, however. God's justice results in grace and mercy. He bends down to scoop up every chip of broken pot. He mends the vessels and offers a second chance to live by the covenant. The picture of transformation represents a return to, or a fulfilment of, the blessings of the covenant promised in Deuteronomy 28:11–12.

The chapter ends with apocalyptic imagery at God's holy mountain, akin to Psalm 18, bringing destruction for Assyria but joy for Israel (vv. 27–33). This links God's promises to Judah with his threats to the nations: both belong to the divine purpose and both involve direct encounter with the living God.

REFLECTION

A living God who never gives up on his people, who waits and waits and waits… Can you, do you, believe this?

TURN BACK!

This chapter usefully combines a summary of the issues of this section, chapters 28—33, in the light of the concerns of First Isaiah (chs. 1—39) as a whole. Overall, the message is a simple repeat of previous oracles: do not rely on Egypt, but on God; do not fear Assyria, but fear God. The Assyrian threat was growing: the crescendo came when Sennacherib invaded Judah in 701BC.

This fourth 'woe' in the series parallels most closely the third, 30:1–5, warning of the dangers of seeking alliance with Egypt and refuge with Pharaoh. Exactly as in the warning to King Ahaz when he sought alliance with Assyria in chapter 7, the issue at stake is not so much political or military as theological. The Israelites do not look to the Holy One in their midst. They suppose that military might is what matters. Despite their covenant status with God, they think and act just like other nations (v. 1). As at 28:29, they are reminded that God is wise—a wisdom that will mean disaster, given all that he has warned (v. 2). In typical Wisdom style, the human is contrasted with the divine, the flesh with the spirit (v. 3), and the creation with its Creator—in order to demonstrate their stupidity and arrogance. The mysterious workings of God are then explained further, through two similes.

Like a lion... like a bird

God is compared, on the one hand, to a lion (v. 4). The lion is hostile, ready to attack Mount Zion. This uncomfortable imagery of God fighting against Zion has developed since the first chapter of the book, and especially since chapter 28. It is not that God is not merciful or does not intervene; rather, it is that Israel has rejected his mercy, which can only result in God turning against his people.

On the other hand, God is compared to a bird hovering overhead, which shields Jerusalem from danger (v. 5). These sheltering wings reverse the picture of God's relation to Jerusalem; they are the opposite of the growling, prowling lion. God is the undisputed guardian of Zion: his protection is stressed with five different verbs for safety. The contrast summarizes a tension that has been evident throughout chapters 29 and 30. Each begins with God attacking or shattering the city, after which a sudden, unexplained reversal takes place whereby God is gracious (29:6; 30:18). The picture is consistent even if it seems contradictory: God fights against Zion, yet also delivers and rescues it.

Some commentators deal with this 'problem' by dividing the text into two sources, one 'original' (the negative aspect) and one 'corrective' (the positive aspect). Historically, this might fit with Jerusalem's remarkable deliverance from Assyria, assuming that the first came before those events, and the second followed afterwards. Another approach is to see in the present form of the text an understanding that is neither unequivocally positive nor negative concerning Zion. The same can be said concerning Assyria, given that in chapters 1—12 Assyria emerges as God's instrument of judgment, the embodiment of his outstretched hand (5:25); yet when Assyria oversteps its role, it is told to expect disaster (vv. 8–9; 14:24–27).

Isaiah's naked appeal

From the beginning of the book, it has been clear that God has a plan and a purpose, for Zion and for the nations. Both God's judgment and his protection are necessary to the fulfilment of this plan—actions that are (variously) directed at both Zion and at the nations. It thus follows that God's lion-likeness and his bird-likeness are not radically different aspects of an unpredictable nature. Rather, they are complementary aspects of an utterly consistent character, evidenced according to the circumstances and requirements of his people vis-à-vis the fulfilment of the plan. God is God: with God is both danger and security. If Judah continues to reject the merciful intervention of God, then utter destruction will be the result. Yet, from the disclosure of God's purpose in creation, there remains an unswerving hope of salvation. The problem is that this hope is incomprehensible to those blinded by folly and arrogance.

Judah's lack of understanding of God was expressed most strongly in 1:2–3. In response, the prophet does not offer a tidy, systematic theology. Rather, he describes the profound struggle of continuing encounter with God. This erupts in his heartfelt appeal of verse 6, the only occasion when Isaiah urges his hearers so directly. Judah has turned away. They must turn back.

PRAYER

God, you are my God. Eagerly will I seek you.

See Psalm 63:1

43

ISAIAH 32:1–20

The NEW KING

This chapter takes a break from the series of woe oracles to broadcast a wholly new era. 'See, a king will reign in righteousness…' This new king is not identified. Rather, the hallmarks of his kingdom are described: justice and righteousness throughout the whole of society (vv. 1–8). The end of the chapter further describes the era in terms of God's spirit coming to the earth and making all things new. The outcome of righteousness will be peace (vv. 15–20).

No more fools and villains

Justice, righteousness and peace encompass the core elements of what Isaiah has longed for, and God has promised, in the future Davidic king (1:27; 5:7; 9:7). Indeed, these are the guidelines for any faithful king. The fruit of justice and righteousness is seen in the care of the poor (Psalm 72:4, 12–14). Through him God's promises of blessing made with Abraham are implemented (Psalm 72:17). The new king is also described as a hiding place from danger, a stream of water in the desert, and a solid rock, offering rest to the exhausted (v. 2). These metaphors suggest that the king will bring well-being and blessing to both individuals and society.

Many commentators take this announcement to usher in the reign of Hezekiah, a 'good' king (according to chs. 36—39), especially given the comparison to his father Ahab. This interpretation would make sense even if Christians might see Hezekiah as a mere shadow for another future king, Christ. But, given that Ahab was named very directly in chapters 7—9, it seems surprising that in this case Hezekiah is not named. The interpretation is peculiarly (and perhaps intentionally) open-ended.

What clearly matters much more than identifying the name of this king is anticipating what will change. Eyes will see and ears will hear (v. 3), suggesting that where there has been comfort, complacency and passive resistance, especially among the leaders, there will be a seeking after God and a renewed responsiveness to him. The topsy-turvy standards of society, whereby fools are thought noble and villains treated with honour, will be revealed and reversed. The hungry, thirsty, poor and needy will now receive the attention they deserve (vv. 3–8).

The problem of complacency

The good news of verses 1–8 will be bad news for those committed to the old era, however. Verses 9–14 address such people in tones of ominous warning. The summons is addressed (several times) to those who are complacent or at ease. Those who feel least vulnerable and most secure are the very ones who are most vulnerable and least secure. Among them, wealthy women are particularly singled out, as if those with the leisure to 'lunch' (expending money earned by the hard work of others) most exhibit the problem of affluence (as also in 3:16–26). Such people need to grieve, since the vineyards will fail and the city will be abandoned (thus the wine will run dry and the restaurants will be deserted)—until…

A spirit from on high is poured out

This spirit (v. 15) grows fruit in the wilderness: not so much grapes for making wine as the fruit of justice and righteousness. Isaiah 40 introduces a section that has more to say about this new era brought about by God. But here is the assurance of comfort and the promise of newness, both in the social world and in the natural world. The latter usually symbolizes the former, and God's work of renewal involves both. 'The problem with Judah's present is that the natural world and the social world are out of joint. The fields and land are fine, but scoundrels govern the country… The subterranean faults must issue in earthquake' (John Goldingay, p. 182).

This new act of creation to restore righteousness results in peace (*shalom*). This is further explained as quietness, trust, confidence, security and rest—for ever (vv. 17–18). This messianic 'for ever' answers the destructive 'for ever' of verse 14. It is eschatological, in the sense that it relates to the future and, ultimately, to the end of history. At the same time, it relates within history to the present realities of the throne of David and the kingdoms of this world. The new king is coming not so much to bring history to an end as to restore justice and righteousness—to transform the world and bring about God's kingdom of peace on earth.

PRAYER

Our Father, your kingdom come, your will be done, for ever.

44

ISAIAH 33:1–24

DELIVERANCE, AGAIN

This chapter completes the series of five 'woes' that began in chapter 28. That familiar beginning belies an otherwise unfamiliar form, however; not least because on this occasion the 'woe' in verse 1 is addressed to an enemy who is not named. Rather, the enemy is described, emphatically, with reference to its treachery and destruction. At 21:2 this word pair was used in reference to Babylon. In the context of chapters 28—32, however, it is usually taken to refer to Assyria. Elsewhere, Assyria and Babylon are viewed in parallel (see ch. 14). It is more important, perhaps, to register the anonymity of the destroyer. Just as with the identity of the new king in the previous chapter, so here the historical application is open-ended.

The woe turns quickly into a plea to God for help (v. 2), illustrating poignantly the attitude of trust for which the prophet has continually been pleading, and the plea is followed by a description of God's exalted position (vv. 3–6). There is a lament of complaint (vv. 7–9) and then an extended description of God's victory (vv. 10–24). Overall, the dominant note is hope, yet the chapter reflects the pattern that has become characteristic in Isaiah: Israel is desolated, God delivers, and finally God's rule is established.

Tradition

Curiously, these themes are all expressed in language borrowed from earlier chapters of Isaiah. For example, the waiting for God in verse 2 echoes God's waiting for Israel (5:2, 4, 7) and Isaiah's own longing in 8:17, as well as their anticipation of the future (25:9; 26:8). There are many other cases, too numerous to list here. And in one place there is a borrowing from the Psalms: verses 14–16 follow the liturgical conventions for entering the temple, such as in Psalms 15 and 24. If a modern author did this, without acknowledging the sources, it would be called plagiarism. Rather, here we must view it in terms of faithfulness to and dependence on the tradition. Either the prophet was so steeped in 'biblical' tradition that he recognized the parallels and described God's work using the same forms of speech, or else the chapter represents the composition of later editors who made sense of God's work through reference to prior categories and experience. Either way, the present is proclaimed with reference to the past, and the future is predicted with reference to what has come before. In other words, the imagination is guided by history. Exactly the same phenomenon is evident in the Magnificat, where Mary borrows words from the Psalms in order to praise God for the new thing he is about to do (Luke 1:46–55).

This technique is called intertextuality, whereby the text points both backwards and forwards. Earlier oracles from Isaiah are reused here to reinterpret the events leading up to the attack on Jerusalem during the reign of Hezekiah. As a result, the past is joined with the continuing experience of God.

Transformation

This technique not only returns to the past to make sense of the present; in the process of reusing a tradition, it also reconceives it and thus transforms it. The recycling of prior material involves reinterpretation. Sometimes, this results in expressions of calamity being transformed into expressions of hope. For example, the tumult of the nations (the 'multitude'), which so terrified Judah at 29:5, 7 and 8, is now heard as the tumult of God's voice (v. 3), which terrifies the nations (and enemy Assyria in particular: 30:30–31). Such transpositions do not deny the previous threat; they underline how such threats do not have the last word. What previously functioned to underline the power of the threat now becomes a resource that lends power to the promises. If this chapter serves to conclude the first half of the book (as some commentators suggest), then its overall message is this: that in the very wounds of God's judgment lie the seeds of hope and wholeness.

God as King

That combination of hope and wholeness is brought about, ultimately, when 'your eyes will see the king in his beauty' (v. 17). This was exactly Isaiah's experience (6:1–7). It anticipates a day when all people will recognize the one who reigns majestically over the whole creation, through the messianic (human) king who serves as his earthly representative (compare 32:1; 40:5–11).

REFLECTION
What would it mean for God to transform your past
into a resource for hope in the future?

DOOM & DESOLATION

This chapter is often paired with chapter 35. The two chapters appear to function as two halves of a whole, chapter 34 summing up the prior material of chapters 1—33 (especially chs. 13 and 24) while chapter 35 reflects what follows in chapters 40—66. They function together as if in reverse correspondence, together summarizing the two major themes of the book: firstly God's judgment over the nations, and secondly God's salvation at Zion. Walter Brueggemann regards chapter 34 as providing 'exaggerated negativity' in the context of the positive, exuberant counterpoint of chapter 35. Certainly, God's anger is raging here.

Chapter 34 picks up, from chapters 13—23 in particular, the challenge to the nations to bear witness to God's sovereign power. As before, this power becomes evident through God's retribution, only here the scope of God's judgment is both wider and deeper. Verses 1–4 transcend the geographical sweep to encompass all nations, and not just all nations but the heavens as well as the earth. And this judgment is projected into an ultimate (eschatological) time frame. For this reason, chapters 34—35 are sometimes called the little apocalypse, corresponding to the longer apocalypse of chapters 24—27.

Focus on Edom

Having embraced the universal horizon, it is a surprise to find the focus then narrowing exclusively on to the destruction of Edom from verse 5 onwards. Edom was Judah's neighbour to the south-east. This long-standing enemy features prominently in the writings of other prophets (see Jeremiah 49, Ezekiel 25, and Obadiah), yet it only received fleeting attention in the oracles against the nations in chapters 13—23 (see 21:11–12). Here Edom functions as a representative of all that opposes Judah, a symbol of hostility that evokes God's wrath. Its destruction is portrayed in the language of the overthrow of Sodom and Gomorrah (vv. 9–10).

The description of the defeat is savage. Edom is described in verse 5 as 'the people I have doomed to judgment'. Here we find what has become the proverbial 'doom and gloom' or 'fire and brimstone' preaching—presented as stemming directly from God. The term translated 'doomed' appeals to the holy war ideology described in Deuteronomy 20, involving the total obliteration of those nations who oppose God and God's people. The image evoked is that of the enemy offered as sacrifice to God, a kind of apocalyptic slaughter. This explains the liturgical activity described in verses 6–8, where a form of *holocaust* (the Hebrew term for the sacrifice of 'burnt offering') is depicted on that 'day of vengeance'. The rhetoric is shocking and extreme—akin, perhaps, to that of various radical terrorist groups known in the 20th and 21st centuries.

Dereliction to the point of extinction

Edom is renamed 'No Kingdom There' (v. 12). Its annihilation is such that its state of nothingness echoes the nothingness out of which God created (Genesis 1:2). This suggests that the land is returned to a pre-creation formlessness, a state of unshaped disorder in which real life is utterly inconceivable unless willed by the Creator.

A further symbol of desolation then extends to the end of the chapter: that of a barren wilderness inhabited by an implausible menagerie of unclean birds and beasts. The list of creatures parallels (and extends) the list found in 13:17–22, which describes the desolation of Babylon by the Medes. From owls to ostriches, and hedgehogs to hyenas, this catalogue is designed to repulse and revolt the reader, especially a reader familiar with purity laws.

The tone of apocalyptic finality is underlined yet again by the repetition of the phrase 'from generation to generation' in verses 10 and 17. There is no mercy to be found from God in this chapter. There is no let-up to the transcendental scene of devastation—until, at least, we read on to the 'partner' chapter of Isaiah 35. For the moment, the reader is called to dwell on the uncompromising obstinance of God. He will not, ultimately, tolerate a challenge to his rule. God's sovereignty is serious business: he will not be mocked. At least, this chapter warns of his furious rage, extending to his decree of a violent fate towards those who do mock.

PRAYER

Lord God, have mercy on me, a sinner—and deliver me from your fearful judgment.

RANSOM & RETURN

Suddenly the imagery undergoes a sharp and joyful transition, from doom and desolation to ransom and return. This transition marks a turning point in the book of Isaiah. What had become, owing to God's fearful judgment, a place of desolation, a place of sulphurous fire, and a place of unclean predators (ch. 34) is now forgotten. God's work of transformation now presents quite the reverse: a desolate place bursting with flowers (vv. 1–2), a parched place teeming with water (vv. 6a–7), and a dangerous place offering safe passage to God's 'clean' people (vv. 8–10).

Singing

The chapter resounds with singing (literally, 'noise'). It is as if all of creation is being amassed and harmonized for a concert: the choir includes the desert in blossom (v. 2), those who were previously mute or dumb (v. 6), and the newly ransomed people of God (v. 10). In each case the joyful noise stems from God's work of transformation, raising abundant blossom, healing disabling infirmities, and ransoming a lost people. In such transformation—where the creation is restored, the needy are healed, and the exiles return—the glory and majesty of God are evident (v. 2).

Just as Isaiah glimpsed God's glory (6:1–3), so now do others. But who are the 'they' who see God's majesty (v. 2)? The word could imply the lush agricultural regions of Lebanon, Carmel and Sharon just mentioned; or, from the last chapter, it might refer to the people of Edom, or even the desert creatures that replaced them. Alternatively, it could point forwards to those with weak hands and fearful hearts, those cured from disabilities in verses 3–6 and, further, to those who return in verses 8–10. Perhaps, all who sing are those who espy the glory of the Lord—for that is why they sing—like the seraphs around the throne (6:2; compare Revelation 4:8).

It is more significant, at this stage, to marvel at the announcement that the glory of the Lord will be revealed at all. Moses longed for a glimpse, but his request was denied him (Exodus 33:18–23). Only Isaiah has been given it, in a situation connected to a unique calling and equipping (ch. 6). Now it is stated that others will also share the experience. This points towards the staggering declaration at 40:5, where it is announced that all people will see it.

Windows on salvation

How people will see the glory of the Lord—precisely where or what they will see—is not directly explained. For example, will they see, like Isaiah did, the hem of God's robe or the flight of seraphs around the throne?

Rather, this chapter presents five pictures of salvation. The first addresses the transformation of the wilderness into a 'bed of roses' (vv. 1–2). The second addresses the feeble, the fatigued and the fearful, encouraging confidence in God's justice and mercy (vv. 3–4). The third announces to those who cannot see, hear, or walk that their disability will be put right (vv. 5–6a). The fourth depicts the hot dry desert bursting with luxuriant springs and swamps (vv. 6a–7). Finally, the fifth picture describes a holy highway along which God's people will return safely to Zion (vv. 8–9).

The prospect of salvation captures the senses and stretches the imagination. It engages with the political realities of exiles returning from Babylon, but it goes far further, into the physical realities of creation and the spiritual realities of the human heart. The climax is not merely arrival at the holy place of Zion, but an everlasting freedom in which grief and pain are overcome by gladness and joy. Clearly this salvation cannot and must not be reduced to a set of simple literal statements.

Indeed, elsewhere in scripture these pictures recur as God's salvation is anticipated and appreciated. It is to the third picture of salvation that Jesus points—'the blind receive their sight, the lame walk… the deaf hear' (Matthew 11:5; Luke 7:22)—when John the Baptist's disciples come to him to establish if he is 'the one who is to come'. Jesus' response not only underlines that we should take these pictures seriously, and literally, as we look for the signs of God's work. It also answers the question of where or how the glory of YHWH is to be seen. He is, indeed, 'the one who is (was) to come'. We see the glory of God most fully and finally revealed in the person and work of Christ.

PRAYER

Lord, thank you for this vision of transformation.

47

ISAIAH 36:1–22

Sennacherib's Intimidation

The previous two chapters, situated at the midpoint of the book and suitably representing its 'core', summarized the messages of judgment (ch. 34) and hope (ch. 35) in Isaiah. The four chapters that now follow are very different in style and interest. They consist of stories concerning Hezekiah, Judah's king, and his conflict with Assyria's King Sennacherib. In many ways they read more like a narrative told by a prophet than the direct message of the prophet himself. Indeed, chapters 36—39 parallel very closely, sometimes word-for-word, chapters 18—20 in one of the historical books, 2 Kings.

The background to chapter 36 involves Assyria's conquest of Lachish and countless other cities in Judah—all save Jerusalem itself. The agitator, Sennacherib, sends his right-hand man (the 'Rabshakeh' is literally his cup bearer or commander; in today's language, his PA) to meet with Hezekiah's representatives and present the challenge. Their place of meeting is suggestive (v. 3): the conduit of the upper pool is precisely where Isaiah met Ahaz in 7:3 to challenge where he placed his faith and remind him to trust God. We may expect the parallel to highlight this subject in reinforcing the contrast between the 'bad' king Ahaz and the 'good' king Hezekiah.

Prophetic parody

The issue of faith is raised by the Rabshakeh's opening gambit. Seeming to imitate the proverbial prophet (he begins 'Thus says the great king', rather like 'Thus says the Lord'), he asks, literally, 'What is this confidence with which you are confident?' (v. 4). It is just the subject with which Isaiah confronted Hezekiah's father in a previous political crisis. In what follows, he stresses the royal representatives' air of confidence, repeating the same key term five times (translated as 'depend' or 'rely')—only the tone is mocking. Here is injury upon insult for Judah: now the classic theme of Isaiah is expounded by an Assyrian. His purpose is not so much to urge godliness and increase confidence as to provoke and undermine. With a patronizing relish, the cunning Rabshakeh then outlines their various strategic options. Reliance on Egypt (v. 6) and reliance on God (v. 7) are both dismissed as inadequate. Judah's own military power is scorned as pitiful and compromised (vv. 8–9). Finally, the Assyrians dare to proclaim themselves as instruments of Judah's God (v. 10), appropriating another of Isaiah's themes: God's capacity to work in and through other nations. As in Isaiah's confrontation with Ahaz, Judah is challenged and cornered, but this time also humiliated.

Political propaganda

This confrontation is heavy with irony for Judah. The Assyrian is only repeating concerns about their strategy and their strength that Isaiah has already voiced to Judah. Isaiah, for example, has already declared that Egypt is too vulnerable to depend on (31:3), but perhaps Judah would or could only hear such warnings in the voice of an outsider, or at the point of extreme need. The irony is underlined by the Rabshakeh's accusation that 'you rebel against me' (referring to his master Sennacherib), when this was the complaint voiced by God at the outset of Isaiah (1:2).

The Rabshakeh's guile takes a new turn in verses 13–20. Hezekiah's men plead for discretion, asking him to speak in Aramaic, not Hebrew, so as to contain his message from the masses. This is grist to the mill for the Assyrian, however. He knows the power of propaganda and, as if intoxicated by his own arrogance, his message simply gathers pace. He casts doubts on Hezekiah, he exacerbates fears for the safety of Zion and he seeks to seduce the people with dreams of a better land. These are familiar tactics in the world of politics.

But the Rabshakeh goes too far. As an outsider, he misjudges the situation with regard to the distinctive land of Judah and the distinctive God of Judah. The land of Judah cannot simply be compared to other fertile land, just as the God of Judah cannot be compared to other gods. He ends up undermining his own regime. Perhaps he imagined a crowd cheering and clamouring for Sennacherib, but instead he finds himself confronted with stony silence, a people who confirm their loyalty to Hezekiah (v. 21).

REFLECTION

Is there a stranger who represents to you your true calling
better than you do yourself?

48 ISAIAH 37:1–20

HEZEKIAH'S TRUST

Chapters 28—32 implied that Hezekiah left a lot to be desired as king, but here in chapter 37 we learn why some may describe him as 'good'. This passage serves as a case study for the faithful actions of a king in a crisis. Indeed, here is inspiration for any godly leader seeking to maintain faith amid conflicting pressures. Finally, at the crunch, we find Hezekiah doing exactly what Isaiah had always urged him and his predecessors to do: to trust God, even when worldly logic suggests otherwise and other places are offering themselves as options. It is ironic, of course, that Hezekiah is turning to God not in response to Isaiah but at the prompt of Assyrian intimidation.

Hezekiah, a role model

First, Hezekiah identifies with his nation's pain. Like his officers who briefed him on the situation (36:22), he rends his clothes at the distressing news. The mockery and insults add up to shame and disgrace for Judah (v. 3), so the king dons sackcloth, as if in mourning, as do those around him. Nothing about his demeanour suggests panic. Rather, we witness a ponderous, measured response. Hezekiah demonstrates both humility and wisdom.

Next, he goes to the house of the Lord to pray, where he bears the rebuke and disgrace before God. The disgrace stems from the way Assyria has ridiculed God—the same disgrace that has marked Judah's contempt of God elsewhere in Isaiah. Hezekiah is absolutely clear that God brooks no rivals, even though his request for the prophet to intercede is hesitant. He speaks of Jerusalem as a remnant (v. 4). In this regard, the prophet is more important than, for example, the priests who are sent to fetch him (v. 2).

Isaiah's response consists of a reassuring 'Do not be afraid'—the same words that were spoken to Ahaz at the upper pool leading to the Fuller's Field in 7:4 as well as in 8:12; 10:24 and 35:4. He then promises that Sennacherib will soon return to his own land, where he will be killed. There is absolutely no need to fear the offender. The prophet provides the king with solid ground for hope.

Nevertheless, the Rabshakeh relays a further message from Sennacherib to Hezekiah, in the form of a diplomatic letter (vv. 8–13). It is anything but diplomatic: it restates his contempt for Judah's God and reinforces his own self-confidence. Following Isaiah's assurance, the speech seems laughable: this is provocation and bullying bordering on ridicule. It repeats the same line, and makes the same mistake, as in 36:18–20. The taunt cites the same destroyed cities as earlier (36:19) and likens the God of Israel to all the other local deities who have proved powerless before Assyria.

Hezekiah follows this message with prayer again, this time in heightened form. He does not appeal to Isaiah for intercession but addresses God directly and immediately. He begins by 'showing' God the letter (v. 14). Then he acknowledges God's distinctiveness (v. 16)—exactly what the Assyrians underestimated—and he points God to the problem of Sennacherib's mocking (v. 17) and the Assyrians' devastation everywhere (vv. 18–19). Finally, he asks God to save Judah, 'so that all the kingdoms of the earth may know that you alone are the Lord' (v. 20). He makes his plea on exactly the grounds that Assyria was set on denying: the distinctiveness of YHWH.

The power of prayer

This prayer is a beautiful example of true faith being brought to voice, and being voiced to the one who is the author and focus of that faith. Note how much of the prayer is about God and his uniqueness: the person praying has little concern for anything but God's name. It is almost as if Hezekiah is reminding himself of how things really are, by telling God what he believes about his sovereignty in the face of pressure to believe in other sovereignties. Dividing the prayer into the three classic components of praise, complaint and petition, we may note how brief is the third section (v. 20a). In these circumstances we might expect Hezekiah to plead more extensively for help. But the request is brief, and how God delivers is left entirely to God. Instead, Hezekiah reminds God of the supreme reason for acting: that the world may come to know that God is God. This is the sole reason for God's action, whether in regard to Israel or the nations, throughout the whole book of Isaiah.

REFLECTION

Think of a troubled part of the world, and what it might mean for people there to know that God is God.

SENNACHERIB'S FALL

Hezekiah's prayer in 37:16–20 is effective: what follows might be seen as God's response. Isaiah has already delivered a decisive promise of salvation, assuring Hezekiah that Sennacherib would never prevail over Jerusalem (37:5–7). Here is further reassurance: a long oracle condemning Sennacherib (vv. 22–29), a sign concerning Jerusalem's future well-being (vv. 30–32), and another oracle reinforcing it (vv. 33–35). Just as the whole saga began with historical background (36:1–3), so it now ends with a note explaining what finally happened. The Assyrians were decimated and the rest retreated back home, where Sennacherib met a sticky end (vv. 36–38).

This second half of the chapter is comprehensive in covering the demise of Sennacherib—with theological explanation, pastoral encouragement and historical account. In other words, it explains why he fails, it offers Jerusalem reassurance through both a sign and a promise, and it details Sennacherib's sordid death.

A contest of hubris versus heaven

The reason given for the fall of Sennacherib is necessity. Just as in the oracles against Babylon and Assyria (chs. 13—14), the end is not merely desirable but inevitable—because he has challenged the Holy One of Israel (v. 23). Success has led to arrogance, and arrogance has led to mockery. Rather than recognizing his place in fulfilling aspects of God's plan (vv. 26–27), he has 'played God', boasting of his own prowess and discounting God's power. The battle between earth and heaven, of an inflated ego pitted against the living God, is depicted in terms of Sennacherib's 'raging' (vv. 28–29). Such 'rage' invokes notions of the thrashing of a frenzied bull—mindless, violent, destructive and pointless. Another word for it is blasphemy.

The issue here is not between two military powers, as Judah was continually prone to understand it, but between God's power and Sennacherib's arrogance. Sennacherib's fundamental problem was self-deception: his own sense of power led him to discount God's power and boast of his own prowess. Isaiah has alluded to this challenge before, and his witness has been shaped to warn the people that God's power and glory are incomparable.

For the sake of David

It is significant that the explanation for Sennacherib's downfall does not include the protection of Jerusalem. God does not bring Sennacherib down *in order* to conserve Jerusalem. Indeed, as Isaiah has already made clear (and for rather different reasons), Jerusalem's days are numbered. Yet here Isaiah presents to Hezekiah a sign from God to assure Jerusalem that it will be safe from the incursions of Sennacherib. This is no instant solution but a future guarantee that after living by faith for a couple of years, during which they recover from the devastation around them, there will be a sense of normality once again. Indeed, the survivors will flourish; the reference to Mount Zion recalls God's glorious plans. Although the recovery seems to follow the normal, 'natural' course of events—there is nothing un-usual about waiting and planting—the community will know that it is the zeal of God that has brought it about (v. 32).

In the condemnation of Sennacherib, God acted for the sake of his name, but in the promise of Jerusalem's protection from Sennacherib, God acts 'for the sake of my servant David' (vv. 33–35). These were just the terms under which Isaiah challenged Ahaz (7:2, 13), recall-ing God's promise to David of an everlasting kingdom (2 Samuel 7). The reference here might serve as a personal encouragement to Hezekiah, as king of the Davidic house. It also affirms how the differ-ing theological traditions—about David, about Zion—come together fully and seamlessly in Isaiah's emphasis on God's incomparable holi-ness and his unassailable plans.

The decisive if disturbing picture of the mysterious and miraculous work of the angel in verse 36 has sparked a debate between super-naturalists and naturalists. Is it a literal description or mythical embellishment? Either way, this chapter testifies to the reality of God's involvement in his world—for the sake of his name, his people, his promises and his plans. He answers prayer and he delivers from danger. Surely this understanding of the events of 701BC thwarts any false confidence or self-deception on the part of Judah? Rather, it invites wonder and gratitude at the power and grace of God.

PRAYER

Lord, rescue those who govern from an attitude of arrogance.

IN SICKNESS & IN HEALTH

Chapters 38—39 function as a pair which, though continuing in parallel with 2 Kings 20, seem only loosely connected to the preceding narrative of chapters 36—37. Verse 6 presumes that the divine rescue of Jerusalem has not yet taken place. If Hezekiah's sickness predates the threat of Sennacherib, this highlights the current placement of these chapters. The reader is being invited to look beyond the particular details of Hezekiah's illness and recovery to realize some wider significance.

Prayer...

The king, weak with affliction, is provoked to fervent prayer by Isaiah's conviction of his imminent death. The 'footnote' in verses 21–22 explains his condition as 'a boil', which Isaiah treats with the remedy of a fig cake. This might suggest leprosy; it was sufficient to prevent Hezekiah from going up to the temple. But these details are secondary. The account is concerned to underline, rather, how Hezekiah responds to Isaiah's prediction with tearful prayer for recovery (vv. 2–3). That he 'turned his face to the wall' perhaps denotes how desperate he was. Reminding God of his faithfulness in the past, and certainly demonstrating his utter dependence in the present, Hezekiah prevails.

Isaiah's second speech underlines how prayer works: it brings God to change his mind. Isaiah tells how God has 'heard... seen... will add... will deliver...'. God gives Hezekiah a further span of life. Furthermore, 'the God of your ancestor David' (v. 5) promises not just Hezekiah's deliverance but also Jerusalem's, with a sign that further demonstrates his sovereignty over time. Perhaps it alludes to the sun standing still, or even receding, as it did in Joshua 10:12–14 when the armies of Israel were given more time to win a victory.

... and praise

The main section of the chapter then relates a 'psalm' that Hezekiah offers to God in response to his healing (vv. 9–20). Significantly, this is not part of the briefer account in 2 Kings 20, suggesting its particular importance in this context for the book of Isaiah.

In form, this verse follows the classic shape of thanksgiving (as found, for example, in Psalms 18, 30, 32, 34; and Jonah 2). That is, it begins with a description of need (vv. 10–12), which evokes a cry of lament (vv. 13–14). Suffering brings the psalmist to God, pleading for attention. Following confession (vv. 15–16), the psalmist recounts God's deliverance (v. 17), and ends with thanksgiving (vv. 18–20).

The last three verses of thanksgiving are especially striking. Up until verse 19, the psalm is voiced by Hezekiah individually; thereafter 'I' becomes 'we'. This marks a shift of focus from the recovery of Hezekiah to that of the wider community of faith. We may suppose that the psalm is presenting a connection between the sickness and recovery of Hezekiah, and the judgment and restoration of God's people. Just as verse 6 extended the effects of Hezekiah's prayer beyond his own personal needs to those of Jerusalem, so the psalm marks the same transition more formally. We may extend the metaphor of being brought back from 'the pit'—a term used in Jeremiah and Lamentations for the experience of exile—from the initial focus on the king to a larger horizon of the whole nation. Thus the psalm points to the possibility of restoration beyond the disaster of exile.

'Lord, teach me to pray'

Constantly through the first 39 chapters, Isaiah warns the Judeans of judgment and urges them to trust the sovereignty of God. Here, at last, is someone who hears and who acts: a king who serves as inspiration and example to his people. In crisis, just when others might be prone to hide from or blame God, Hezekiah turns to God.

The inspiration of this chapter concerns prayer. Hezekiah demonstrates why he prays and how he prays. He prays with the conviction that all of life depends on God. It lies in God's hands to end life or extend life. It lies in God's hands to bring threat or to bring rescue. There are no contradictions here, because God is the one who gives life in the first place, the one who knows all things and causes all things and claims all things. In all circumstances—in judgment, in the face of death, in exile—God is the place to turn. And God is the one who hears... and sees... and adds... and delivers.

PRAYER

Give thanks to God for an answered prayer, following the thanksgiving pattern of verses 10–20.

The WORD of the LORD IS GOOD

Continuing from chapter 38, this chapter is even more striking in its function as a 'bridge' between First and Second Isaiah, linking the very different material relating to exile in chapters 40—66 with the context of Judah in chapters 1—39. On the one hand, like the preceding material, it concerns King Hezekiah in Judah (late eighth century), and on the other, it anticipates the incursions of Babylon and subsequent exile (sixth century).

Merodach-baladan was king of Babylon during the years 722–710 and again from 704 to 703. It is likely that it was during the later period that he sent envoys to Hezekiah (as in ch. 38, apparently preceding the siege of Jerusalem described in chs. 36—37). Perhaps this approach was to establish an alliance in the face of the Assyrian crisis that faced Babylon as much as Judah. Given the different casting of this incident from its parallel in 2 Kings 20:12–19, however, we conclude that what matters here is the reference to Babylon. This future superpower comes to dominate the life of Judah. The passage paves the way for the transition from Assyrian defeat to Babylonian capture.

All is exposed

Hezekiah seems to welcome the envoys gladly, even if a conducted tour of his treasures and armaments seems unusual and, with the benefit of hindsight, perhaps foolish. The text does not criticize, however; it merely stresses how Hezekiah revealed everything. In the context of Isaiah, we might understand this to suggest that the king takes pride in his material assets, rather than trusting in God. Despite all we have witnessed of his faith in the previous couple of chapters, Hezekiah repeats the sins of his father Ahaz. In reality, despite these riches, Hezekiah is utterly exposed and vulnerable.

What may have been a relatively innocent (and insignificant) visit is now freighted with the hindsight of history. The irony of the situation makes us gasp: Hezekiah has invited the future arch-enemy to come and 'case the joint'! Yet the king is not condemned by Isaiah. The prophet merely stresses how the Babylonians have seen everything, and uses the incident to foreshadow the future.

Every item that Hezekiah has shown the envoys will be hauled off by them, as well as some of his own sons as eunuchs (v. 7). This not only implies the end of the temple and other riches in Jerusalem—riches that will be transferred to serve a foreign regime and foreign gods (as described in Daniel 1). It also alludes to the end of the royal line. Through his actions with these Babylonian envoys, Hezekiah unwittingly prefigures the end of the Davidic monarchy and the exile.

The announcement of exile is not new, but the reference here is more direct. There is no room for ignorance or misunderstanding. The 'reminder' of exile here, at chapter 39, jerks the reader into a new mode of anticipation, involving certainty as well as concern.

'The word of the Lord is good'

Hezekiah barely draws breath before he replies to Isaiah's declaration. Is he in denial, is he smug or selfish, or is he genuinely welcoming a word of truth, even if it is foreboding? There may be an element of each of these responses—especially, perhaps, given that the judgment will not affect him personally but only those after him. At face value we may take it that here is an acceptance of God's sovereignty. Hezekiah appears to embrace the future with an understanding of God's will—a will that unfolds according to a plan.

Even in this 'final' chapter, it seems that Hezekiah remains a model of faithfulness according to Isaiah—a good king of Judah. Nevertheless, he is human: mixed motives may be imputed with regard to his treasure and his trust. These motives are not explicated, however: the text retains a respectful silence, as if this is not the focus. Rather, the interest lies in engaging God's people, and Isaiah's readers, with the realities of exile. This word of God redefines the future. As in the last chapter, what may once have been a straightforward narrative about the king now functions to foreshadow events for his subjects.

Like Hezekiah, we are invited to say, 'The word of the Lord is good', whatever the circumstances—peace and security, or exile. This was Isaiah's conclusion, following his near-death glimpse of God's majesty. This is Hezekiah's conclusion, following his near-death experience of illness and siege. This will be Judah's conclusion, following the near-death lesson of abandonment in exile.

REFLECTION

*Can you say, 'The word of the Lord is good',
whatever the circumstances?*

HERE IS YOUR GOD

For some readers the opening words of Second Isaiah will be so familiar from Handel's *Messiah* that it is hard to appreciate their original context in Isaiah. After 39 chapters sustaining an overall message of fearful judgment, suddenly we begin a hopeful phase. The tone is gentle: the first word is 'comfort', reassuringly repeated, and addressed in the most personal terms to 'my people' from 'your God'. This God continues to speak tenderly, with the news that the punishment is over and their sin forgiven.

This comfort is not a future promise but a present reality, which implies that the punishment alluded to in the last chapter for subsequent generations (39:6) is being depicted here as current. We do not know whether Isaiah son of Amoz wrote these words for a situation 150 years later, or whether God called a new 'Isaiah' during the exile. Either way, the message brings readers to make a dramatic transition as they read the book in its received form. In the mind's eye we are transported to Babylon, where we identify with people who know the pain of suffering. Thus, to hear the very address 'Jerusalem' stirs the heart concerning an abandoned place and a broken relationship.

God's highway

The comfort consists in the big news that God is due to appear. The God whom Isaiah was privileged to glimpse in glory (6:1–7) is going to reveal that glory to all people everywhere (v. 5). This will be a major public occasion, for which the preparations must be extensive. On the human level, Israel is being prepared by the experience of exile. With regard to the landscape, valleys will be raised up and mountains flattened, to create a direct route—a straight and level highway—rather like when building a railway or motorway. This visit warrants the red carpet treatment: all nature and all people are on standby. When the big moment comes, all flesh will witness the revelation.

'Flesh' is indeed an appropriate term, for the effect of this climactic moment establishes a proper perspective on humanity compared to divinity. The people are literally stunned. Not only are they lost for words but they wither like grass and fade like flowers (vv. 6–7): they can't cope in the face of such glory! The word of God and the breath of God, by contrast, are constant and unbending (v. 8).

Heralds of good news

Judah is used to bad news, not good; surely the experience of God's judgment instinctively elicits fear at the prospect of his coming. Yet the prophet urges them not to fear (v. 9): God has already assured them that their penalty is paid (v. 2). Rather, in excitement they should run up the nearest hill and shout from every mountain-top—until, presumably, the mountains are levelled to create the highway. They are to be heralds (an image depicting women proclaiming the news of a military victory around the community) of the gospel. Their message of good news is simple: 'Here is your God!' (v. 9). This gospel expresses the presence of God in a situation—in Babylon—exactly where he seemed to be absent. And, one might suggest, it is delivered by those of whom one might least expect it: women!

Verses 10–11 expand on the nature of the God who is here. On the one hand he is a victorious warrior, and, on the other hand, he is a caring shepherd. According to the first image, God's outstretched arm guarantees Judah's victory as in 14:27, and he brings recompense—booty—as if paying back a debt. God's sovereignty is final, and his majesty is expressed through unsurpassable power. At the same time he is like a shepherd—a royal image of guardianship subverted in a radical, tender, maternal care for all who are vulnerable. He will cuddle the young lambs in his own arms. This juxtaposition of power and gentleness, or majesty and mercy, mirrors that experienced by Isaiah in chapter 6 as well as by Israel in the exodus (compare Deuteronomy 1:30–31). Yet it reverses normal expectation.

This section of chapter 40 is well known, not only thanks to Handel, but also thanks to John the Baptist. He was in the wilderness, enacting the text by embodying the very voice crying out, when he quoted verse 3 (Matthew 3:3). He thus rekindled the decisive gospel of these verses for a subsequent generation in exile. He directed those assembled to see the glory of the Lord, declaring, as Jesus approached for baptism, 'Here is your God!'

REFLECTION

How do you cope—how will you cope—in the face of God's glory?

LIFT UP YOUR EYES & SEE

Everything that follows in chapter 40, from the announcement at
verse 9, describes the God who is here. It is as if, in the depression
and despair of exile, the people have suffered a loss of memory and
imagination, but now they should lift up their eyes and see. Here is
a reminder of who God is and what he is like. In a sense, verses
12–31 expand on the two contrasting figures of conquering warrior
and gentle shepherd (40:10–11), images responding to the twin
needs of Israel in exile. On the one hand, they need vision and conviction to counter Babylonian claims; on the other, they need confidence and encouragement to tackle their own needs.

In a nutshell, this passage tells us that God is:

* the perspective beyond the universe (vv. 12, 26).
* the wisdom behind creation (vv. 13–14).
* the power before all nations (vv. 15–17).
* the strength beneath all weakness (vv. 27–31).

What is more, this God is available to give all these gifts—perspective
and wisdom, power and strength—to his people again.

Who is like God?

God is so vast as to hold oceans in his palm and stretch heaven along
his arm (v. 12). God is so wise as to lie beyond counsel or instruction
(vv. 13–14). God is so strong as to weigh islands like dust on a
shopkeeper's scales (v. 15). The result is that the nations are simply
nothing before him: by implication, even the intimidations of
Babylon are sheer emptiness (v. 17).

In case comparison still seems viable, verse 18 invites nominations
for a kind of divine beauty contest. There follows an amusing description of the making of an idol. It is intricate, fiddly and costly; and in
the end it is a joke because the idol is liable to topple, just as Dagon
toppled continually before the ark of the covenant (1 Samuel 5). God
is without peer: he cannot fall over because he sits above the circle of
the earth. He brings princes to nothing (v. 23) as readily as he
summons the stars into existence (v. 26).

The way that seems hidden

In verse 27, Isaiah quotes the people's lament: their way is hidden and their rights are disregarded. The same cry could echo from war-zone refugees or oppressed minorities anywhere in the world, feeling forlorn, ignored, trampled. Isaiah responds not with sympathy or publicity but with argument! He declares the crazy folly of imagining that the people of God might drop out of God's notice for one moment. How could they pass out of the love and care of the God he has just been describing, who keeps the world in being and breathes life into every creature? He hasn't forgotten them. Indeed, he's passionate about them, so passionate that this shepherd gives himself to be what his people need. He gives power to the faint and strength to the powerless. He gives his own life to his ailing, flagging people and promises that if they wait for him they will be reanimated with his own breath.

The word 'wait' (v. 31) includes hope and patience and trust. Those who wait for God are those who trust in him, relinquishing their own little plans and leaning on him with all their weight. Isaiah is urging all Israel exactly as he urged Ahaz earlier—to faith (see ch. 7). If they can look to God rather than depending on their own strength, then, unlike Ahaz, they will be renewed with a strength that is not native to them. Their urgent demands will be met with resources beyond their own—so they can run and not be weary. The shepherd provides for each member of the flock according to their needs. Unlike those (such as the Babylonians) burdened with 'gods' or idols that must be carried, this God does the carrying (40:11).

The message of comfort for the exiles is that God, the all-powerful Creator, is coming back to Zion. As a result of the message, they are urged to see (v. 26) and hear (v. 28) afresh—and therefore to trust. Previously the problem among God's people was not only lack of trust; it was also blindness and deafness. Has exile taught them to see and hear? Then they must act (see Ezekiel 33:30–33). In this case, to act is to trust.

REFLECTION

What gift do you most need from God?

Do Not Fear

How many times does 'Do not fear' need saying to fearful people before they cease to fear? The phrase recurs three times (vv. 10, 13, 14) within a whole chapter that consists of ongoing reassurance from God to his terror-stricken people. Clearly, these people take a lot of reassuring. For, to Israel-in-Babylon, the past is shameful, the present is horrific and the future looks completely hopeless. The Israelites betrayed God's promises, and are punished for their sin. Their city has been destroyed, and a great chasm of desert lies between them and their holy land. Meanwhile, a new superpower threatens from the east: even in Babylon their future is not secure.

Summoned to trial

Verses 1–7 pick up the challenge of reassurance boldly. Israel's God, YHWH, takes up a seat in an imaginary courtroom and invites the nations to appear for a public adjudication. This is a legal summons, aggressive and adversarial in tone. God launches an inquisition: 'Who has roused a victor? Who has done this?' (vv. 2, 4). No response is recorded. Unchallenged and undaunted, God expounds his own supreme sovereignty with regard to a victor from the east. Later named as Cyrus (44:28; 45:1), this king of Persia is renowned for his military prowess. Audaciously, God claims that it is he who calls Cyrus, he who asserts his control over every form of human activity in history from the beginning of creation to its end. It turns out that the nations are not only silent; they are terrified. They resort to fashioning idols in self-protection, images so pathetic that they need fixing down to prevent them from falling over (vv. 5–7; compare 40:20). Suddenly, the tone of God's voice softens. It is as if, while delivering a verdict, the rhetoric has been interrupted by a distant whimper, a cry of pained curiosity—wondering if this all-powerful high-court judge still has a place in his heart for the child who failed him.

I have chosen you and not cast you off

Turning and bending down, God addresses Israel—'you'—fondly as 'my servant... whom I have chosen... my friend' (v. 8). The God who is the first and the last (v. 4) recalls those whom he first called, Abraham and Jacob. He repeats himself, in case Israel didn't hear the first time, affirming that he does not regret his choice of Israel from all the farthest corners of the earth. Indeed, he continues to choose Israel (v. 9). The Israelites may have felt rejected and been punished—and they may have rejected themselves—but God has not rejected them. Perhaps the people are so depressed, their self-image has sunk so low, that they can't hear it or believe it. So the tender shepherd's love song continues, and he urges them three times not to fear. Firstly, they should not fear, given how powerful, how victorious, is God's right hand, as he has just explained (vv. 10–12, compare vv. 1–7; 40:10). Secondly, they should not fear because they themselves are held by God (v. 13; compare 40:11). Unlike foreign idols, they cannot topple (compare v. 7). Thirdly, they should not fear, however worm-like they may feel owing to the humiliation of exile (compare Psalm 22:6), because 'your Redeemer is the Holy One of Israel' (v. 14).

This is a staggering assertion. The title for God is borrowed from First Isaiah—grounded in Isaiah's distinctive vision of God's holiness (ch. 6) and signifying the threat of judgment—and then turned on its head. The God who is king over all the earth, the hem of whose robe could barely fit in the temple and whose holiness demanded that even seraphs protect themselves: this great God is Israel's redeemer. A redeemer (Hebrew: go'el) is a technical description for the family member, the next-of-kin, who serves as a legal guardian, responsible for protecting you in poverty or debt, injustice or danger. In extreme circumstances the go'el is responsible for freeing the relative from slavery. Here it is asserted that God is Israel's next-of-kin: Israel need not fear because God undertakes to fulfil the commitments of this relationship, whatever resources it requires to defend Israel from danger and restore Israel to freedom.

If Israel can cease to fear, they may begin to dream again—to conceive the new age, and share in God's creation purposes (vv. 15–16); to imagine the transformation of creation (vv. 17–20), when all may finally see and know the Creator. But first, can they begin to see and know him again?

REFLECTION

'You are my servant; I have chosen you and not cast you off' (v. 9).
Do you believe this?

55   ISAIAH 41:21—42:9

MY SERVANT... MY DELIGHT

The pattern of this text mirrors the last. It begins with another court scene where God challenges his rivals to argue it out (41:21–29). It continues with a moving account of God calling and investing in his servant (42:1–9); finally, it ends with a vision of the transformation of creation (42:10–17). The overall thrust continues to be assurance for exiles: a reminder of who is in control, of what he plans and of where his people fit in.

The gods are summoned but it seems that they have nothing to offer concerning the past or the future (41:22–24, 28–29). By contrast, it is repeated, God has stirred up a conqueror ('one from the north' is often taken to be Cyrus, like 'one from the east', 41:2, 25) and given a herald of good tidings to Zion/Jerusalem (40:9: 41:27). The Creator God demolishes the claims of other gods and then demonstrates his commitment to restore his exiled people. Here is the big picture—and an unconquerably big God—followed up by the personal picture, and a deeply personal God.

'Here is my servant'

In 41:8 and 9, God called Israel 'my servant'. It is logical, therefore, to suggest that the one who causes God to celebrate in 42:1 ('my servant, whom I uphold, my chosen, in whom my soul delights') is a collective reference to God's people Israel. As before, God's commitment to this servant is affirmed. Further, he is now invested with God's spirit to undertake responsibility. His task is to bring justice to all nations. He undertakes this work silently and peaceably (quite unlike the conqueror of 41:25). Most importantly, he will not give up until he has established justice throughout the earth (42:1–4).

This description of the servant's task resonates with the task of Israel described elsewhere. That 'the coastlands wait for his teaching' (42:4) echoes the vision of nations streaming to Zion to learn God's teaching and receive his justice, in 2:2–4. It is as if God's servant is now charged to implement God's plan.

Although no one other than Israel is named as the servant in Second Isaiah, there remains much mystery regarding the identity of the servant. These verses, along with three other passages that focus on God's servant (49:1–6; 50:4–9; 52:13—53:12), known together as the 'Servant Songs', have commonly been studied in isolation from the rest of Second Isaiah, as if originating elsewhere. Despite disproportionate efforts to establish a historical identity of the servant other than Israel, there has been little success.

The problem is that several individuals are designated 'God's servant' in scripture: for example, Isaiah (20:3), Eliakim (22:20), David (37:35), even Nebuchadnezzar (Jeremiah 25:9). The term 'servant' is not so much a technical term as a general description of any faithful person under God, so it is used of patriarchs, priests, prophets and kings as well as Israel. It is more significant here that the emphasis lies on the servant's role, his method, and his achievement—and on his relationship to God. He acts unobtrusively, on behalf of those who are fragile and distressed, until justice is complete. The ministry is costly, yet it does not fail. Meanwhile—indeed, before the task is even outlined or executed—this servant is described as bringing delight to God.

New things

The verses that follow may be taken to explicate further the work of the servant, even though the images are different. The powerful Creator God (42:5) commissions the servant, in language redolent of Moses and the exodus traditions (42:6; compare Exodus 6:2). He is charged to be 'a covenant to the people, a light to the nations', thus embodying a covenantal relationship beyond Israel itself to the nations. In practice, this involves the opening of eyes, the releasing of prisoners and, more generally, transforming darkness to light. Assuming that it continues to relate to Israel, this commission goes far beyond 41:8–20 to resonate with the vision of chapter 35. Israel is chosen, but not simply for its own sake. It is chosen for a purpose. Privileges and responsibilities belong together.

When did the new thing declared here (42:9) come about? The answer is not straightforward. While engaging with the Old Testament context, Christians also hear the declaration echoing in the New. At Jesus' baptism, a voice from heaven quotes 42:1, along with a messianic reference from Psalm 2:7. At the point where Jesus is commissioned, so he is identified as both Servant and Messiah.

REFLECTION

Meditate for a few moments on God delighting and investing in you.

A SERVANT DEAF & BLIND

Verses 10–17 follow up the servant's call and commission with a liturgy of praise and thanksgiving. It is as if all creation rejoices at the work of God's servant. The first four verses (vv. 10–13) read like selected highlights from the Psalms (especially Psalm 96), with exclamations of praise to God from the ends of the earth, because of who he is and because he reigns. The second four verses (vv. 14–17) offer thanks for what God is about to do. Until now, he has not intervened to end Israel's exile. But now he will do a new thing: he will scream like a woman in labour, not holding back his concern for Israel. Once again we hear of God making rough places level and railroading a new route through the mountains and wilderness (compare 40:3–4; 41:17–20). The details and specificity of the return journey about to be 'birthed' increase with each repetition. Those guided home are described as blind (underlining their helplessness) but not forsaken (v. 16). They are led from darkness to light; that is, so long as they trust God. This victory is theological, for others—notably, those who trust in sham images, like the Babylonians—will find themselves left behind (v. 17).

Listen, you deaf; look, you blind!

God's change of plan (42:9, 14) is the more remarkable given what follows from verse 18. The servant, in whom God delighted and in whom he invested (42:1), turns out to be blind and deaf. He sees but does not observe; his ears are open but they do not hear—despite the call and commission he has just received. The agent of healing needs healing himself. This could be the result of war wounds, the tragedy of exile having so damaged Israel that it can no longer raise itself to fulfil God's purposes. Or it could represent a fulfilment of God's call to Isaiah to 'stop their ears, and shut their eyes, so that they may not… turn and be healed' (6:9–10), the result of Israel's long-standing sinfulness. Either way, there is a question mark concerning the servant's ability to serve.

It follows that before the promise of salvation is pursued further (in ch. 43), it is appropriate to address the adequacy of the divine judgment on Israel's past (vv. 21–25). God purposed the exile 'for the sake of his righteousness, to magnify his teaching and make it glorious' (v. 21). Has this punishment served its purpose? Because of the people's sin, Jacob was spoiled and Israel robbed. Yet, in spite of all this, the people did not walk in God's ways or obey his law (v. 24). In sum, the judgment of exile did not bring about repentance. As verse 23 puts it, there is still no desire to listen for the time to come—to trust in God and God alone.

We may conclude, then, that God's judgment did not achieve its desired effect. God brought about the exile because of human sin. Yet now we hear him announcing an end to exile, despite human sin. There has been little change with regard to human sinfulness. It is just the same in the story of the flood. God blots out his creation because of human wickedness (Genesis 6:5, 11). Yet at the end of the flood he promises never again to destroy the earth, despite human wickedness (Genesis 8:21).

A God of grace?

It is sometimes said that the Old Testament portrays a harsh God who delights in punishing his people. Certainly, it portrays a stubborn people who continually invite punishment. Here we find that God has decided not to punish his people further, despite their resistance to the lesson of exile.

It is remarkable that, nevertheless, God describes his wayward people Israel as his servant, his chosen, his friend (41:8). On the one hand, the servant is deaf and blind; and on the other hand he is God's dedicated one (v. 19). Furthermore, this servant—the one in whom, it is said, God delights (42:1)—is called and commissioned to represent him and fulfil his plan. God's purposes involve mending broken things; and to do this, he calls broken people. Indeed, perhaps it may be through the servant's very brokenness that healing can take place (42:3; 2 Corinthians 4:7–11).

REFLECTION

Do you recognize God bringing healing to others as much through your brokenness as through your strength?

57   ISAIAH 43:1–13

And I LOVE YOU

A chapter beginning 'But now...' demands that first we recall what preceded it. The previous verse expressed God's fury with his people Jacob-Israel. The whole of the last section (42:18–25) depicted the utter hopelessness of their situation, being unteachable even through the experience of exile. Though retaining the title of 'servant', God's servant turns out to be blind and deaf to God—thus, we might suppose, completely useless for doing God's work.

We are led to expect a declaration of despair, an epilogue of abandonment. Instead of the 'therefore' of logic, however, we find a 'but now' of reversal. God pledges himself again to his people, not because they deserve it or have earned it; simply because he is God, a gracious God. This vow of commitment begins at the beginning. The God who created heaven and earth, whose universal creative scope has been extravagantly expounded from chapter 40 onwards, also created Jacob and formed Israel. Whereas 'created' echoes the elegant work of the transcendent God who began with nothing (Genesis 1:1), 'formed' suggests the intimate modelling of the immanent God who sculpted clay (Genesis 2:7).

Do not fear

God reassures his people with another 'Do not fear' (vv. 1, 5; see 41:10, 13, 14), this time on the grounds that he has redeemed them. He is their *go'el*, the family member who has acted to rescue them from danger and slavery. It follows, of course, that he knows their name (what's more, he uses it—indeed, both of them!). As a result of being redeemed, they belong to him (v. 1). He is with them even in the floods and fire of the punishment that they have brought on themselves (v. 2; 8:5–8; 42:25).

Then the love song moves from the theme of redemption to ransom: the price paid to cover a debt or release a hostage. It seems likely that verse 3 refers to the ransom God paid in the past, as evidence that he will pay the ransom in the future (v. 4). What God did at the Red Sea, bringing Israel out of Egypt (Ethiopia and Seba are regarded as part of southern Egypt), he assures Israel he can and will do again. God responds head-on to the needs of a people with low self-image, who feel dishonoured and unloved: 'You are precious in my sight, and honoured, and I love you.' He proves he means it by pointing to past events and assuring them that he would do the same again.

In case Israel didn't hear it earlier, in case they forgot from the time before—and just in case they have the capacity to believe it now—God repeats, 'Do not fear, for I am with you' (v. 5). The assurance of God's presence is the barest essential—perhaps the only thing that really matters. Israel may be focused on getting out of Babylon, but, regarding the future ransom, God's horizon is wide, encompassing east and west and north and south. It includes 'everyone who is called by my name, whom I created for my glory, whom I formed and made' (v. 7, echoing v. 1). The regathering presupposes an Israelite centre, yet it extends universally. What God plans for the future far exceeds what God did in the past.

You are my witnesses

Verse 8 returns to Israel's blindness and deafness. Such problems do not go away simply because of God's love and commitment. Israel is brought to court, where the nations also gather to debate their insights into 'the former things'. We might expect Israel to be shamed before the world, but rather it is the nations who are challenged, and God's people who are called to act as witnesses. How remarkable—for the blind and the deaf to be appointed witnesses!

Still more remarkable is that God, at the point of Israel's hopelessness and despair, is not only declaring his love and commitment, but also enlarging their role in his plans and purposes. Not only are they 'my servant whom I have chosen' (v. 10) but they are to be witnesses in a legal case concerning God's omniscience and omnipotence—to prove that God has no rivals. We may expect that the purpose of this court-case is to bring the nations to acknowledge God. Rather, it is 'so that you may know and believe me and understand that I am he' (v. 10). Through witnessing to the nations, Israel themselves may come to see and hear. This is faith seeking understanding; or, getting oneself involved so as to find convictions resolved. It is as we hold out God's salvation to others that, by God's grace, we ourselves are saved in the process.

PRAYER

Thank you that you love me, not because I am good
but because you are God.

DO NOT DWELL *on the* PAST

Having extended Israel's horizons far beyond the circumstances of Babylon, verses 14–15 now return to Israel's own need of rescue from the Chaldeans (Babylonians). The full range of Isaiah's titles for God is brought together here. He that is Creator of the heavens and the earth, and King above all (as Isaiah discovered for himself, 6:1), is also King of little Israel. The Holy One of Israel, whose holiness meant judgment for sin (6:5), is also their Redeemer. God's servant can rely on its master—a servant has to—for God works both creation and redemption. Indeed, the two are inseparable in Second Isaiah.

A new exodus

This God announces an act of deliverance that will be far greater than the former time. Careful reference is made to the original exodus from Egypt—the demonstration *par excellence* of God's redemptive power. He 'who makes a way in the sea, a path in the mighty waters, who brings out chariot and horse' (vv. 16–17) will act to deliver again, and this new act of deliverance will far exceed the old.

Despite the detail reminding us of the first event, Israel is urged not to remember the former things. Despite the emphasis elsewhere in Isaiah and throughout scripture on remembering, indeed on structuring all of life around, what God has done in the past (for example, Exodus 12:14)—for this is how we learn what God might do again—Israel must look to the future. Perhaps the people are living in the past, when what is required is a facing of the future. Even though there is continuity from past to future in terms of the way God acts, the past must serve as a resource for what the future may hold, not as a curb to the imagination. For the future is bigger than the past.

Now a way in the wilderness (v. 19) succeeds the way in the sea (v. 16). Initially we picture the return journey from Babylon to Jerusalem, but the 'new things' seem to stretch horizons far beyond any isolated sixth-century perspective. The picture of the wild animals honouring God (v. 20) hints at God's cosmic new creation, the peaceable kingdom of the final days (ch. 11). The God who welcomes the deaf and blind servant will certainly renegotiate the defining events of history. And all of this will end, as depicted in the book of Revelation also, with creation responding to its Creator, with God's people declaring God's praise (v. 21).

Ransomed, healed, restored, forgiven?

Just as we begin to picture Israel skipping through the wilderness and singing praise to God on their way home, the tone changes from hopeful new beginning to continuing old critique (vv. 22–28). Throughout these early chapters of Second Isaiah there has been a constant flip-flop between assuring Israel and confronting Israel, between declaring hope and facing reality.

We find a court scene again; only this one is unusual: it is the only one where God opposes Israel. This time God is defending himself against Israel's persistent complaint of being disregarded (compare 40:27). He responds with counter-accusation. Despite the fact that God has not burdened Israel with the demands of ritual sacrifice (not possible in Babylon, with no temple), Israel has become weary of God. The servant has not been serving; rather, he has needed to be served. God has been carrying the servant—not in the sense of renewing his people, as promised (40:31), but in the sense of being burdened by the weight of their sin (v. 24). The point of sacrifice was to express repentance and seek forgiveness, which is just as valid in Babylon as in Jerusalem (v. 25).

Perhaps we may now understand why it is that, throughout these chapters of Second Isaiah, the community seems more ready to believe in God's judgment than in his mercy. It's a common cry: that God is too often and too easily perceived as a harsh judge, not as a gracious loving father. But when his people keep their distance and persist in foolish ways, like the prodigal son in a far-off land, they can only imagine his frustration. History has shown, and Second Isaiah testifies, however, that when people do find the courage and repentance to turn back and seek him once again, they hear not the sharp rebuke of judgment but the gentle tones of welcome. Their Creator-Redeemer might be heard saying, 'You are precious in my sight… and I love you' (43:4).

PRAYER

Lord God, visit those in exile today, and lead them to freedom.

I WILL POUR OUT MY SPIRIT

A pattern of reality checks is emerging in the 'forties' of Isaiah. On one hand, there are the acknowledgments of Israel's quiet despera- tion, with an analysis of the backdrop of sinfulness, circumscribing life in Babylon. On the other hand, there are the affirmations about God and his glorious assurances to his people, embroidered through the cloth with continuous golden threads. Both represent reality. Even though it is hard to embrace the two, both persist: Israel's resis- tance to God and God's commitment to Israel.

'But now...'

Chapter 43 (like chapter 42) ended with the former reality, a depress- ing court disputation that highlighted the persistent failure of Israel for generations. If there was ever any hope in human progress, 43:27 puts paid to it. Then comes chapter 44 beginning (as also in ch. 43) with a resounding 'But now' (see also Romans 3:21). It presents the other reality again. It reminds Israel that there is more to their story. This is not to deny what has happened, but to offer an alternative per- spective and, indeed, an exciting possibility. Verses 1–2 repeat and summarize the key themes of assurance so far: Israel-Jacob is God's servant and God's chosen. And God is both Creator and Redeemer: the one who formed this people out of dust will save them from oblivion. Thus Israel is urged for the seventh time, on the basis of God's nature and commitment, 'Do not fear'.

These reminders pave the way for introducing a new dimension of grace. God's people need not fear because he promises to pour out his spirit on their descendants. As a result, their offspring will receive blessing (v. 3). This gift of the spirit is like the pouring of water on dry land. The picture of a desert flowing with streams of water has recurred in Isaiah concerning the future (see 30:25; 32:2; 35:6–7; 41:18–19; 43:19–20). It produces a burgeoning of luxuriant growth (v. 4; compare 35:7), precisely reversing the effects of judgment which laid waste the land and destroyed the crops (1:7–8; 24:4–7).

What does this imagery of growth infer? The idea of numerical growth would be especially striking to a dwindling Israelite commu- nity. The promise of progeny—descendants like the stars in the sky and the sand on the seashore (Genesis 22:17)—was an important aspect of the original promise of blessing to Abraham. But verse 5 underlines a dimension of spiritual growth, whereby God's people 'own' their commitment to God and do not hide their true identity. To say 'I am the Lord's' suggests, in particular, an understanding that they belong to God. This has been the case ever since God brought them out of Egypt and invited them to make a covenant with him at Sinai (Exodus 19:5: 'you shall be my treasured possession'). But it is underlined by a new understanding of God as Redeemer, for, in technical terms, the redeemed belong to the one who redeems them. This verse may also be taken, more radically, to offer a hint concerning another sort of numerical growth: through 'adoption'. Is it that non-Israelites may come and be 'converted', so as to be joined to God's people and included in the covenant? If so, this would fit with the vision of 2:2–4 and 14:1. Third Isaiah will return to this theme of foreign people coming to acknowledge the God of Israel (see 56:3–8; 60:10–14; 66:18–21).

Who is like me?

Verse 6 lists another series of familiar epitaphs affirming the nature of God—King of Israel, Redeemer, Lord of Hosts, the first and last (compare 41:4)—building a picture of his complete incomparability. This is underlined by the challenge God throws out, the seemingly rhetorical question, 'Who is like me?' (v. 7). The context is disputation again, to which Israel is called once more (following an eighth 'do not fear') to be God's witnesses (compare 43:10). Israel is requested to bring evidence from its own experience and history of who God is. There is only one rock—a designation for God that draws on the song of Moses (Deuteronomy 32:4, 15, 30–31), a testimony to God's foundational work with Israel at the exodus (deliverance), in the wilderness (faithfulness) and at Mount Sinai (covenant).

The pouring out of God's spirit results in a renewed understanding of God's people—that is, people belonging to God—such that they are renamed and rebranded as 'the Lord's'; and it underlines their call to be his witnesses. Here is a magnificent Old Testament foreshadowing of the Christian understanding of baptism.

REFLECTION

To whom do you compare God?

RETURN *to* ME

In 44:7 God dared to invite speculation as to 'who is like me?', challenging Israel to respond as witnesses to what he is like. The section that follows (vv. 9–20) demonstrates to those who witness how idols are made just how different are these so-called gods from the one true God.

Home-made gods

This passage is rather different from the elegant poetry of the surrounding material. It reads as something between poetry and prose —perhaps an ancient equivalent of Hilaire Belloc. It represents a cross between social critique and doggerel, demanding to be read tongue-in-cheek. It is playful, making fun of the images of gods and pouring scorn especially on those who make them. With regard to Israel, it subtly underlines the demands of the second commandment (Exodus 20:4–6) and undermines those who do not follow it. This is a tonic—perhaps the most effective tool of all—to help Israel not to fear (44:2, 8 and so on) and, moreover, to trust again in the one true God (compare 43:22).

The focus of the portrayal consists of some practical instructions, a parody of some DIY tips, for making gods. Like a Blue Peter programme, or a Dorling Kindersley guidebook, it starts with the finished product and works backwards. It begins by focusing on the artisans and their tools (vv. 12–13)—the blacksmith in the smithy, the carpenter in the woodshop—offering some human-interest details along the way. After arriving at the first stage of the process, the planting of a tree (v. 14), it pauses to reflect on the usefulness of wood as a material for heating and cooking as well as for worship (vv. 15–20). The point about its household 'convenience' is well made, skilfully exposing the domestic limitations of anything made from it.

That is the beginning and end of the matter (vv. 9–11, 18–20): these gods are simply bits of wood. However carefully they are crafted, they are no different from that which is burned to make a fire. They may have eyes but they cannot see; their minds are shut so they cannot understand. Reverberating in the background is the analogy with God's people (1:3; 42:18) but also the utter contrast with God, who sees and knows (40:28; 41:17). But—and this is the greatest joke—no one who makes the idols realizes this. Perhaps these people are not even consciously conspiring against God: they are so stupid that they turn for help to the very objects they themselves have made!

The details of how idols are fashioned makes for an uncomfortable read: such painstaking description suggests the likelihood of first-hand observation. Living in Babylon, the Israelites were prominently surrounded by such practices. Evidence suggests that they were not only tempted to worship Babylonian gods, but that some were tempted to make images of YHWH in like manner. Although idols are ultimately nothing, those who make them and worship them will pay for it. Especially for those who are called to be witnesses to God, such behaviour is an abomination (v. 19), since it misleads people about the true nature and identity of God (v. 20).

'Return... for I have redeemed you'

God is not mentioned anywhere in the foregoing 'diversion' about making images. In verses 21–22 his voice is suddenly heard again, naming Jacob-Israel as his servant and reminding them that he made them, not the reverse. They are called to remember and not forget these things—these key assertions of Second Isaiah—even if they are among those who have made idols. God's forgiveness, first sounded in 40:2 (compare 43:25), is announced again, prefacing the heartfelt plea (the most direct exhortation in the chapter) to 'return to me'. God has redeemed his servant unconditionally, but he now pleads with his beloved willingly to return the gesture of love and commitment.

Meanwhile, the whole cosmos sings with joy at God's salvation of Israel and the glory he purposes through it (v. 23). It seems that the heavens and the earth, the mountains and the trees make good witnesses. Can Israel do the same?

REFLECTION

Of what things are you tempted to make idols? Can you
acknowledge how pathetic they look next to the
Creator of the universe?

CYRUS, *the* ANOINTED SHEPHERD

This is a pivotal moment in the prophecy of Second Isaiah: Cyrus is
named as the deliverer of the exiles. At 44:28 there is a turn from the
general to the particular, from affirmations concerning what God is
like to explanations of what he will do, from the realm of eschatological hope to the reality of historical time. God forms and creates, he
stretches and spreads, he frustrates and turns back (44:24–25), and
now God says… that Cyrus is his shepherd and that Jerusalem will
be rebuilt (44:28). God declares Cyrus as the means of fulfilling his
divine purposes. God will intervene in the world to free the exiles,
restore Jerusalem and rebuild the temple. The linking of the latter two
themes is a new idea that becomes increasingly important in later
chapters of Isaiah.

God's new David

Addressed to Israel, the acclamation concerning Cyrus as God's
shepherd would be surprising, to say the least. The term 'shepherd'
carried connotations of a king who cared for his subjects personally,
associated in particular with David. In 40:11 God announced that he
himself would serve as shepherd. Not only does the God of Israel use
foreign nations to deliver punishment to Israel on his behalf. Now he
appears to be delegating the role of restoration to a foreigner—the
king of Persia.

This is even more striking in 45:1, where Cyrus is referred to as
'his anointed'. In later usage this term refers to the long-awaited
Messiah who will deliver Israel at the end time (translated into Greek
as 'Christ'). More commonly, it refers to the consecration of Israel's
kings (1 Samuel 12:3; 24:6), even their priests (Leviticus 4:3) and
prophets. In this context it further associates Cyrus with David,
suggesting that what God originally intended to do through a king in
the Davidic line, he will now achieve through this pagan ruler. Only
David has previously been described as 'anointed' and 'shepherd'.
The anointing makes abundantly clear that Cyrus is specially designated for a divine commission. This involved enacting God's plan of
salvation. God has grasped his right hand so as to equip him to
subdue nations and strip kings—in other words, to shatter Babylon.

Israel's sacred tradition is being boldly reapplied. Israel will be saved by a non-Jew, a Gentile! This work is done 'for the sake of my servant Jacob, and Israel my chosen' (45:4): God's central purpose remains the people he has chosen and called. Yet just as God calls his people by name (43:1), and 'surnames' those on whom he pours his spirit (44:5), so he calls Cyrus by name and 'surnames' him—even though Cyrus does not even know God. He will come to know him, for the overall goal is that all people, from east to west, will come to the knowledge of God (45:6). As ever, God's focus on the salvation of Israel is the means to a larger end: that Israel may carry God's salvation to the world. In the meantime, God can and does use people who do not know him, who unwittingly fulfil his purposes even without realizing it. The king of Persia may have been looking to expand his empire, but God had even more expansive plans.

Weal and woe

The sovereignty that all people will come to acknowledge one day is then stated in the most sweeping language we have seen so far (45:7). Through the contrasting word pairs of light and darkness, and weal and woe (more literally, peace and trouble), God not only claims the credit for making light and peace; equally he confesses to creating darkness and evil. YHWH of Israel takes the responsibility for everything, including the darkness and suffering that have come to Israel, to make the point that there is no other. They cannot blame other gods, nor can they escape to kinder gods, because there are none. The logic of monotheism is that we turn to God in good times and bad, because he alone holds it all. There is nowhere else to go. What follows in 45:8, however, affirms that God's ultimate creative purposes are for light and peace, not darkness and evil. It reads as a prayer: God's own commission for the cosmos to start overflowing with the righteousness and blessing that he always intended for creation. This imagery of abundance, with the heavens raining blessing and the earth sprouting fruitfulness, is also found elsewhere in the Old Testament (see, for example, Hosea 10:12; Malachi 3:10–12).

PRAYER

Thank you, Father, that you work through strangers and show the Church your purpose even through those who don't believe.

EVERY KNEE SHALL BOW

The declaration in the last section (44:24—45:8) about a Persian king as God's anointed—despite the joyful affirmations concerning God's overwhelming sovereignty and his intentions for righteousness—seems to be just too much for Israel. Verse 11 here suggests that Israel responded with protest. We can almost hear their murmurings: 'What is the world coming to? Does God have no concern for us?' Apparently Israel is set in its ways: it wants to be saved in its own way. Uncomfortably, this turns out to be different from God's way.

The potter, the parent

We only witness one side of the conversation: God's response to Israel's complaint. He hears it and replies—this is not the kind of complaint that falls on deaf ears—but it is a robust response that puts Israel firmly in its place. By means of two pictures (vv. 9–10), God points out to Israel that the created is entirely dependent on its Creator. Firstly, clay is powerless to form itself; it becomes something only through the hands of the potter. Secondly, a baby cannot determine its father at conception, or its mother during birth. The pot and the babe both exist through means entirely beyond themselves: they have no power to determine their own life or form.

Yet a baby grows up, finds its own voice and complains, forgetful of the grace by which it was made and seeking to take charge of its own future. It is for just such an attempt at self-determination that Israel is roundly rebuked by its potter-parent-God, and reminded that 'I made... I created...' (v. 12). Through Cyrus, the Creator God proposes to rebuild the city and set his exiles free (v. 13), but the exiles seem to be fussy about how they are freed. It is rather like a starving person, when offered white bread, saying, 'No thanks, I prefer brown'. But God is not moved by this complaint: he will not be swayed from his overriding commitment to liberate. He hears the complaint but does not give in (unlike when Abraham complained in Genesis 18), because he has wider concerns beyond Israel that Israel seems consistently reluctant to address.

Israel versus the nations?

The rest of chapters 45 and 46 continue with familiar themes concerning the uniqueness of YHWH and the absolute reliability of the future in his hands. This serves as an ongoing summons to shun idols and to put faith in God, even though the present may feel uncertain. One element that emerges out of this case for the universality of God is the place of Israel in his care, relative to that of other nations. It is emphasized that the idol makers will affirm that God is God (vv. 14–15): indeed, all the ends of the earth are invited to turn to God and find in him their salvation (vv. 22–25). God is a universalist: his concern encompasses the whole world and he longs that all people would come to know him (compare 2:1–4; 19:16–25; 25:6–9). What, then, of God's particular commitment to Israel? Is Israel a nation whose salvation now apparently depends on a foreigner?

There are tensions to this debate. Verse 14 can be read to suggest that foreign nations will come to Israel to make supplication to it because they see that God is there in a special way. They will come to Israel on Israel's terms, and pay homage. This underlines the glorious re-establishment of Israel (thanks, presumably, to Cyrus' victory) whereby Israel appears to gain credit and receive blessing. The promises made to David and to David's line (which were, at least partially, applied to Cyrus) retain their relevance for Israel as a whole.

God's promise to Abraham that through him all the families of the earth would be blessed (Genesis 12:3) underpins the other side of the debate. The special place God holds for Israel—which Second Isaiah continually affirms—is not an end in itself, but an illustration of the relationship that God longs for with all humanity and the means by which he hopes to achieve it. Verses 18–25 underline this wider commitment. He is not elusive by nature (v. 19; compare v. 15): he has revealed himself to Israel so that through Israel God's righteousness might be recognized universally. In other words, God's election of Israel is instrumental: Israel is called for service. By implication, therefore, his commitment to Israel is provisional. One day the nation's service will be complete and its calling fulfilled—when 'To me every knee shall bow, every tongue shall swear' (v. 23).

PRAYER

Lord, help us understand the place that Israel and the Jewish people continue to have in your purposes.

BEASTS *of* BURDEN

Given the repetitive, rhetorical style of Isaiah, we may conclude that the audience was slow to respond. That assumption is stated here explicitly, where Israel is addressed as 'you transgressors' (v. 8) and 'you stubborn of heart, you who are far from deliverance' (v. 12). Perhaps the prophet is close to his wits' end as he continues to tackle the problem of idols and the incomparability of God.

Bel and Nebo

For the first time Cyrus was named at the end of chapter 44; now for the first time two of the Babylonian gods are explicitly named (v. 1). These two were prominent deities, carried in the annual New Year's 'parade' with great ceremony from one city to another. The prophet's description here makes a mockery of such a procession: these 'great' gods are no longer lifted high but stooping, no longer revered by pilgrims but lugged by donkeys. Like a used Christmas tree, once beautiful, they are now passé, and fit only for discarding. This is a story of decline and fall.

It is designed to humiliate those who worship such gods, especially those who might recall for themselves a journey into captivity, when the contents of their temple were carried off before their own eyes (v. 2). This is not a specific prediction about the fall of Babylon so much as a comment on gods that need to be carried. How can a god that you have to carry around with you ever save you? At a time of crisis, such gods are an added burden, for they are heavy and need to be carried out of harm's way. This contrasts with the God of Israel, who not only does not need to be carried, but carries his people from the womb to the grave (vv. 3–4; compare 40:28–31). How can the Israelites possibly think of comparing God, who stands outside creation, with idols who only exist within it (vv. 5–7)?

The very naming of Bel and Nebo adds another dimension to the critique. Undermining Babylon's gods—especially the 'lord' of the gods, Bel (or Baal), and the son of Marduk, Nebo, patron of the royal dynasty—is a way of undermining Babylonian power. Just as YHWH legitimates Israel and Israel's future (if the people will only let him) so these gods 'legitimate' Babylon. But Babylonian power, like these gods, is mere cardboard. If only they could see it for what it is! This kind of rhetoric is designed to empower the Israelites, so that they might believe in their deliverance and trust in their God, whose reality cannot be compared to glitz. If they could only see and not remain blind, then they might realize how powerful they are and how powerless are the Babylonians who hold them captive. Such seeing demands them to look beyond appearances, however, and to recall their testimony, so that they may trust again in God.

Memory: the antidote to unbelief

The prophet challenges the community to face the truths about God in a summary of his sovereignty (vv. 8–11), recalling his deeds of the past, his foresight concerning the future and his faithfulness in delivering that which he has promised. In a situation of need, it is natural to look to outside help, whether the military or the miracle. But the resources the Israelites require are not external to them; they lie within their own tradition, if only they care to mine it. In the very phrase 'I am he' (v. 4), there lies the reminder of the unchanging God of Abraham, Isaac and Jacob, who heard the cry of the slaves in Egypt and equipped Moses to lead them out (Exodus 3:13–15).

The chapter concludes not with a theoretical treatise on monotheism, but with an evangelistic proclamation of good news (vv. 12–13). Paraphrasing, the megaphone declares, 'Listen, you stupid idiots! God is going to save you! When? Soon. Where? In Zion.' God has purged Jerusalem of its filth (4:4) and is setting there a crown of beauty that will draw all the nations to it (4:2; 44:23; 62:3). 'Stop stooping and scraping. Set down those heavy loads. And start to dance!'

PRAYER

Lord, help me to see through the trappings of human power
and remember your sovereignty.

PRIDE & FALL *in* BABYLON

The previous chapter undermined the legitimacy of the gods of Babylon. This chapter completes the dismantling of the power structures, with a taunt to unseat both leaders and citizens. The poetry focuses on Babylon's arrogance, personifying 'her' as a woman whose fortunes are to be reversed. There is a double reversal, for in 1:8 it was the personified city of Jerusalem that was to be abandoned and desolate, and in 3:24 her beauty that was shamed. Now it is the turn of 'Miss Babylon'. The prophecy purports to be addressed to Babylon, but we may assume that it is the exiles who receive it and relish it. The story that has been (so far) a tragedy is becoming more like a pantomime, where the oppressors are now in line for oppression.

From riches to rags

The exalted princess is reduced to a humble peasant. She who lived the luxurious life, tender, elegant and dressed in finery, is humiliated and shamed, charged with menial tasks and exploited sexually (vv. 1–3). The rhetoric is pointed and merciless, even though it imitates a cry of lament: the oppressed clearly enjoy the idea of their oppressors being brought low. They only pretend to grieve: the tears are a cover-up for excitement. This is an imaginative construal of the fall of Babylon, associated with and attributed to the Holy One of Israel (v. 4). The now-familiar divine view of history is repeated (v. 6), just in case there are those with any lurking convictions concerning Babylon's power. Babylon did not 'seize' Judah and Jerusalem. Rather, God gave his people into Babylon's hands because he was angry with them for squandering their inheritance.

Now God is angry with Babylon, for the way 'she' has treated his people. She has not acted with justice—she has not shown mercy to prisoners of war—and thus now it is the Babylonians' turn to bear God's reproach. God expects mercy of all nations, perhaps especially towards Israel. The superpower should have known that its power was not unlimited, that the one to whom it was finally accountable is a God whose final account concerns mercy.

In the style of all mockery, the poetry dwells on this reversal with a satisfied wringing of the hands. As if to underline how pride precedes a fall, Babylonian over-confidence is detailed at length. The underdog sees it plainly. The Babylonians presumed that their pre-eminence would endure (v. 7), they supposed that prosperity insured against loss (vv. 8–9) and they shrugged off any accountability for their actions (v. 10). It is as if they are self-consciously imitating God: 'I am, and there is no one besides me' (v. 8; echoing 43:11; 45:5, 6, 21; 46:5, 9). The prognosis for such an invulnerable approach to life is not promising. Evil and disaster strike without warning (v. 11). Not only do the Babylonians lack the insight to prepare for it; they also lack the power to resolve it and appease it—thereby demonstrating that they are far from being like God. Babylon's punishment will match its pride. The elegant city-figure will lose all that guarantees her security in traditional society: her husband and her children.

Babylon's false claims to authority and glory are founded on false knowledge (vv. 12–13). Babylonian religion has already been undone (ch. 46). Now the remaining ideological resources of the empire—their technology and learning—are also disarmed. The sorcerers and magicians are given short shrift, for their enchantments consistently bring wrong counsel (v. 9). Those who scan the stars to predict the future are also misguided, and can't even save themselves. It is as if they wander aimlessly because they are staring at the sky instead of looking where they are going. Nothing will prevent the loss that lies ahead (vv. 14–15), because no one is immune from God.

Babylon, symbol of oppression

This is not a historical anticipation of the precise way in which Babylon will fall. Rather, chapters 46 and 47, taken together, present two testimonies to the imminent destruction—the self-destruction—of oppression. They are complementary taunts that transform dominance to impotence, and fear to contempt. They address one particular historical empire, but they also speak to representative 'Babylon', 'you who show no mercy', as developed in Revelation 18.

This is powerful propaganda in the hands of powerless Israelites. If it is the word of God, then the speaking of it, in itself, undermines false legitimacy and contributes to bringing a nation down. So, once again, the gift of this prophecy urges Israel to trust God.

THINK

When does judgment represent good news?

65 ISAIAH 48:1–22

PEACE—*but* NOT *for the* WICKED

Standing back and reviewing the overall movement and shape of Isaiah, we can see that this chapter marks a transition. It concludes the prior chapters (chs. 40—47) of Second Isaiah, focusing on deliverance from Babylon through Cyrus, and it introduces another section (chs. 49—55) in which a new figure becomes central and the interest moves increasingly to Zion/Jerusalem. After verses 14–15, Cyrus receives no further mention, and nor do the other main concerns of chapters 40—47: the critique of idols, the defence of God's superiority and the rousing of wayward Israel. But in this chapter, the problem of wayward Israel reaches a climax. When Israel was in the wilderness following its rescue from slavery, the only obstacle to realizing freedom proved to be the Israelites themselves. So now in Babylon: the only remaining obstacle to Israel's rescue from exile proves to be the Israelites themselves. It is time for confrontation.

God's stubborn people

Chapter 48 begins with a summons to 'hear' (v. 1), which is repeated three further times (vv. 12, 14, 16). To hear is to heed, to understand, to obey. Previously the people had been deaf to God (42:18–19). They never heard God's plans (vv. 7–8). Now God takes them by the scruff of the neck to shake them and stare them in the eyes until they listen. He speaks harshly and directly, even while reminding them that they are the house of Jacob, those called Israel, those who swear by the name of YHWH and who aspire to his character (vv. 1–2). The modern reader is invited to stand with Israel and hear this pointed address too. 'You are obstinate, and your neck is an iron sinew and your forehead brass' (v. 4). The essential problem is that Israel fails to acknowledge its God, continuing to turn to idols (vv. 5, 12–13). Israel is refusing to assume its task as witness to God's deliverance (43:12), despite the dramatic contrast between the former things and the new (vv. 3, 6; compare 43:19). God's anger is unrelenting, even though his grace is also unrelenting: 'I defer my anger... so that I may not cut you off... My glory I will not give to another... I am the Lord your God' (vv. 9, 11, 17). The real tension between God and Israel has become overt. Previously the court scenes pitted Israel's God against the Babylonian gods (41:1–7, 21–29; 43:8–13); now the battle-lines are drawn closer to home. God speaks as directly to Israel as he did to Babylon in the previous chapter. The situation is so bad and the prospects are so good: how is it that God's sovereignty over history is still doubted?

At the very beginning of Isaiah, God described his people as rebellious children (1:2). Despite exile, nothing has changed (v. 8). Despite their unhappiness, God neither insists on his way nor desists from loving them. He does not cease to parent them, though the cost, in terms of anger and pain, is very great.

The Lord God has sent me

After a glowing confirmation of the role of Cyrus in performing God's purposes (vv. 13–14), there is a sudden and unforeseen change of direction (v. 16). It is marked by a change of voice to the first person pronoun, presenting significant challenges for interpretation. Who is the 'me' whom God has sent and endowed with his spirit? Is this the autobiographical voice of the prophet behind Second Isaiah? Or is it a new voice, who is not fully introduced and whose mission is only defined later, at 49:1–6? At this stage, the task of the anonymous figure is to deliver an oracle from God, beginning at verse 17. It affirms, 'I am the Lord your God' and defines future goals: to teach the people of Israel for their own good, and to lead them in the way. This 'way' is the path out of Babylon (see, for example, 43:16, 19; 45:13), though it also carries a moral dimension (for example, 26:7; 40:14). The reference to instruction, and to the commandments (v. 18), underlines the principle understood throughout scripture that blessing is related to Torah, to keeping the law. Perhaps it is fitting that this emphasis on obedience is followed by an exuberant shout of joy concerning God's deliverance from Babylon and his provision for those who return, as at the first exodus (vv. 20–21). However, the chapter ends with further warning. There are those who may exclude themselves from God's joy and peace (v. 22).

REFLECTION

Is our problem that God has not given us enough, or that we have not embraced all that God has given us?

SALVATION *to the* ENDS *of the* EARTH

As in 48:1, this chapter opens with the command to 'Hear!' This is not the voice of God but an 'anonymous' voice speaking, and it is not addressed to Israel but to the coastlands and nations far away. The message has global implications: 'that my salvation may reach to the end of the earth' (v. 6).

You are my servant

In verses 1–3, the person who speaks introduces himself—but without revealing his name. The imagery he uses—called by God, named in the womb, mouth like a sharp sword—is reminiscent of Jeremiah's call (Jeremiah 1), suggesting a prophet. The central declaration, 'You are my servant, Israel, in whom I will be glorified' (v. 3), allies this figure with God's call to Israel as servant (42:1, 19; 44:1; 45:4). Indeed, the parallels with 42:1–4, 6 are striking.

Yet here is an individual speaking. Is it that this individual is called Israel—somehow to represent in his person the corporate body that has already been called as a servant? Alternatively, is a new double appointment being announced here: 'you are my servant; you are Israel'? If so, then we may suppose that an individual figure is now appointed to the role of servant, whether in place of or to supplement the servant-work of Israel which has borne the title up to this point. Given that the nation Israel continues to bear the title and role of servant, yet continues to fail in performing its chosen role (48:1–2), we may suppose that here God is naming some further servant, an individual, to embody faithfully that which Israel could not. Even this servant perceives himself to have failed (v. 4)—perhaps in delivering the summons to depart from Babylon (48:20–21). Nevertheless, God confirms his call and vindicates him, in the sense that the servant's justice ('cause') is identified with God's rule of justice (v. 4).

In part, this servant is given a role similar to that of Israel: to be a light to the nations and a covenant to the peoples (vv. 6, 8; compare 42:6). There is one key aspect that is new: to exercise a ministry to Israel (vv. 5–6). This part of the role is described as 'a light thing', as if restoring Israel is a mere fraction of the full vocation of this servant. Being a light to the nations—establishing God's justice on earth—

will involve far more than Israel's particular needs, but it does include them.

Many scholars have assumed that this 'servant song' follows from the first so-called (42:1–4) and have sought to identify the mysterious servant figure independently of the present context. Yet the mystery of his identity seems to be just the point: the person behind the voice that speaks in verses 1–6 (as also in 48:16) is carefully concealed. What is more significant is the fact that God is designating a human agent to bring about healing and restoration in the whole world, and particularly with reference to Israel. At this point, we may imagine, Israel is left guessing as to who this agent might be. In the early Church, with the benefit of hindsight, he became identified with Jesus, and Jesus' ministry became that of the Church.

Slave of rulers

In verse 7, Israel is described as the servant of rulers, as if to emphasize the problem with their call as servant of God. At the same time, God's continuing call to his chosen Jacob-Israel as servant is underlined, despite their failures. In verse 8 he reaffirms that this 'slave of rulers' will become 'a covenant to the people', a repeat from 42:6. God has a continuing commitment to Israel as servant, despite the new call to an individual. One does not replace the other; neither do the two clash. Rather, they share God's servant call, even while developing it in complementary directions.

Israel's particular role is expressed in relation to the homecoming from Babylon. Israel will be a covenant to the people through re-apportioning the land and freeing the prisoners (vv. 8–9). God promises to feed and protect the prisoners on their journey home (v. 10; as during the first exodus, 48:21). There will be a highway through the mountains, and comfort for God's people (vv. 11, 13; language and imagery repeated from 40:1, 3–4), as if to underline that the good news concerns the particularities of Judah's circumstances, even while also hinting at a wider homecoming that reaches to 'far away' places (v. 12; compare vv. 1, 6).

REFLECTION

What is the 'light thing' that God has called you to? And what is the weightier thing to which he might be calling you now?

FORSAKEN & FORGOTTEN?

Chapter 48 marked a transition within Second Isaiah. God's people Jacob-Israel are now addressed as Zion, and the focus has moved from Babylon to Jerusalem, from exile to restoration. In 49:14, however, a complaint is voiced by Zion, a complaint that underpins the whole of the passage that follows. It is not new: it was first voiced at 40:27 by the people then known as Jacob-Israel. It is a desperate cry from a still-desperate people—'YHWH has forsaken me, my Lord has forgotten me'—a cry of abandonment that echoes liturgically through the book of Lamentations (compare Lamentations 5:20). Their self-image is at rock-bottom. The crisis of confidence—despite the new name of Zion and the new focus on Jerusalem—continues unchanged. The idea of the heavens and mountains joining together in song (49:13) seems to have washed over them. Never mind the cosmos rejoicing: its inhabitants are miserable.

God's response is urgent, gentle, wise: 'he' is depicted with maternal imagery. Just as it is improbable that a mother could forget her newborn babe, so it is unthinkable—nay, impossible—for God to forget his beloved people. He nurses them to his breast; his compassion is endless; they are inscribed on his palms; he holds them continually in view (49:15–16). He will never forget his children; nor will he be their debtor. 'Your builders outdo your destroyers' (49:17). In other words, in so far as they may be compared in magnitude, the blessings will outdo the sufferings. They will be repaid, and with extra. God's response outdoes Zion's complaint. God's fidelity will mean an end to exile and a joyful return. As before, Zion is instructed to look up and see (49:18; compare 40:26; 42:18). The promise of restoration is imaginatively unveiled before her very eyes, through various different tableaux.

Orphans?

An enduring image of judgment has been that of a city turned to hollow ruins and haunted by wild birds and beasts (13:19–22; 34:12–15). Now the picture of Jerusalem is quite the reverse (49:19–21). Vast throngs of children descend, as if a Pied Piper is playing—more than the city can embrace, more than she realized she had borne. Mother Zion is far from barren. She is overflowing with the blessing of Abraham, with offspring as numerous as the grains of sand on the seashore (compare 48:19; Genesis 22:17). Furthermore, the imagery underlines the relation of city to inhabitants, like that of mother to child: Zion protects and gives prosperity to her offspring. They are far from forsaken or forgotten.

The next tableau (49:22–26) reacts to the perception of the children of Israel as cheap labour, helpless captives who are abused in the hands of their oppressors. As if the world's rulers are waiting for the divine umpire to raise his hand and signal the start of a sports event, these children will be carried home—cradled in arms, riding piggyback or lifted high on shoulders. Forsaken and forgotten? No chance. They will be treated like royalty, and the world's kings and queens will vie to care for them, to grovel and serve them. If this seems too shocking, too impossible, then imagine, at the command of the Lord, the greatest lion dropping its prey or the harshest tyrant handing over his captives as readily as an obedient retriever returns the hunt to her master's feet. Such is the unrivalled sovereignty of God, and such is his concern for his children. He is the Lord, and he is their Redeemer.

Divorce? Reconciliation?

The theme of the mother and her children continues in the final section (50:1–3), depicting a debate between God and his people that gets to the heart of the matter. Whose fault is the exile? It is as if a truth and reconciliation commission has been set up. God is accused of divorcing his wife unjustly and then maliciously selling his children into slavery. God defends his role in the family breakdown: the problem did not lie with him. It was not that his love had grown cold, but that they had grown wicked. And God has not abandoned them: they are not forsaken and forgotten. He longs to re-establish the family and be reconciled. His hand is keen to redeem and his power is able to deliver. But when he came, as promised, to bring Zion's deliverance, no one responded; when he called, his people did not answer.

PRAYER

Lord, deliver me from self-pity, and give me a grateful heart.

WEARINESS & WAKEFULNESS

A personal voice speaks up again 'out of the blue', which we may presume to be the same individual 'I' as that of 49:1–6 and 48:16. At 49:3 he was identified with the servant and with Israel. He was given the task of regathering Israel and the task of being a light to the nations (49:5–6). The latter stands in continuity to the task that Israel was given earlier (42:1–9). Thus, this individual servant picks up the mantle and either shares in or takes over from the mission of Israel as servant, at the same time as pursuing a mission for Israel itself. God has called this servant by name (49:1), yet he is not identified in Isaiah by name. Some suppose that this 'I' is the prophet himself speaking, though there is no corroborating evidence. Meanwhile, the anonymity of the servant is maintained; and following the speech, it is simply confirmed that this was 'God's servant' speaking.

The servant explains that God has equipped him to teach, so that he 'may know how to sustain the weary with a word' (v. 4). This servant is keen to serve, and he has a strong sense of stewardship. He is eager to use the gifts God has given him to fulfil the purpose for which they were given. He wakes up 'morning by morning' to attend to God. He has 'open ears' and is hungry to be taught, so that in turn he may nourish others (vv. 4–5). The gift of teaching begins with being teachable and being taught. The contrast between this servant and Israel could not be much greater. He longs to respond to God, whereas Israel did not answer when God called (50:2). He longs to hear, whereas Israel was deaf (42:18–20; 48:8). He longs to be taught, whereas Israel resisted God's teaching (48:17–18). He longs to teach others, whereas Israel has consistently overlooked its responsibility to others, both the needy close to home (1:17) and the nations in God's plan (2:3).

I have set my face like flint

The core of the matter is that there is no hint of resistance about the servant (v. 5), despite persecution, whereas the people of Israel were rebellious before exile (1:2) and have continued to rebel during exile (48:8). They have not learnt their lesson, whereas the servant is keen to learn all he can, even in the face of opposition (v. 6). The counterbalance to Israel's rebellion is the servant's sense of grace. He mentions the struggle: 49:7 suggests that he was despised and abhorred, and 50:6 describes violence, insult and humiliation. But he does not dwell on it. Instead he dwells on God, describing all that the 'Lord God' (literally 'YHWH sovereign') has done: giving him the tongue of a teacher (v. 4), opening his ear (v. 5) and helping him (vv. 7, 9). His early morning times of learning with God have brought about his formation quite apart from any information: he has the depth of character to accept the experience of suffering and shame. The servant has set his face like flint, immovable in his focus on the God he serves and in his dedication to fulfil the call to service. Thus he trusts absolutely that God will vindicate him (vv. 7–9), even though it has not happened yet.

Sustaining the weary

The final two verses of the chapter relate the speech and its significance to Israel. Verse 10 endorses the servant as an inspiration to Israel for trust, obedience and reliability. It also suggests that fearing God involves obeying the servant. Such is the nature of the servant's work and teaching for Israel and for God that to obey the servant is to follow God. If it is the servant's task to deliver Israel from exile, then surely Israel must follow him to find deliverance. Thus the servant's word will sustain the weary people (v. 4), through suffering to vindication (vv. 7–9).

Nevertheless, the phrasing of verse 10, and the warnings of verse 11, suggest that the people of Israel continue to be preoccupied with their own sense of abandonment (compare 49:14) and are unwilling to move on. If they could only trust God in the darkness, they would be sure of the light beyond (compare 9:2), but they prefer to try kindling their own lights. The fire that they have created turns into their torment.

PRAYER

Lord, free me of resentment and let me serve you with joy.

In the SHADOW *of* GOD'S HAND

This passage rings with language that will, by now, be familiar from earlier chapters of Second Isaiah. God continues to work at encouraging and empowering his people, but the task of raising their confidence and extending their vision—of clothing them with strength —is seemingly endless. Back at 40:1 God promised comfort: here it is reasserted twice (vv. 3, 12; see also 49:13). Yet again the people are urged to lift their eyes and look beyond their current circumstances (v. 6; compare 40:26; 49:18). They are reminded of God's plan to bring teaching, justice and light to Gentiles (v. 4). They are commanded three more times to listen (vv. 1, 4, 7; compare 49:1). They are prompted with the power and possibility of God (vv. 9–10). They are reassured that there is no need to fear (vv. 7, 13; compare 41:8–16). They are named and claimed one more time: 'you are my people' (v. 16; compare 40:1; 43:1). And this passage goes further in depicting the joyful day of salvation, to which Israel can look forward (vv. 3, 11). But first, Israel needs to look back.

The rock from which you were hewn

The secret for looking forward is to look back (vv. 1–2, 9–10, 13). What God has done before, he can do again. Looking to the rock from which they were hewn and the quarry from which they were dug is to trace the beginning of their family tree. It is to identify their bloodgroup, track their genes, understand their identity, claim their foundation, inhabit their story. They are not rootless, even if they are currently homeless. From 'nowhere' God called Abraham, and promised blessing in the form of descendants and land. He and Sarah would give birth to a great nation. These promises were preposterous! Because the old couple were nomads, the prospect of owning land was ridiculous. Because they were elderly and barren, the idea of bearing children was laughable. The promise to be a great nation was every bit as impossible, humanly speaking, as God's promise that Israel in exile will be a great nation again. But God called Abraham and, thanks to his obedience (despite a few hitches), God blessed him and made the one into many. Now God is calling—and comforting—Zion; he longs to bless her and transform barren desert into fruitful garden. And this will be not just any backyard, but a garden like Eden (v. 3), filled with joy and gladness, thanksgiving and singing. The future will be like the past—except that it will be better.

Just as the promises to Abraham hung on his obedience, so these promises demand cooperation. They hang on Israel's heeding the call (v. 4). No longer does God's plan of blessing to the nations, involving the work of his servant in bringing teaching, justice and light to the distant coastlands, hinge only on corporate Israel. God has appointed an individual to represent Israel and fulfil this work, to them as well as for them.

Wake up! Wake up!

Suddenly Israel does start to look back, recalling God's great work in 'days of old' according to stories of creation and redemption (vv. 9–10). Israel is harnessing the past, but to reminisce and grieve—as if everything has changed, as if God needs to be aroused to come to their aid, as if he needs to put on his strength like a piece of clothing. Here is a *cri de coeur*, a lament expressed in the language of Israelite history mixed with colourful Babylonian mythology (sleeping gods, raging monsters and watery chaos). It may illustrate a confused exilic mindset, or a profound conviction concerning God's sovereignty over Israel and the nations, fusing into one continuous sweep his work from creation to salvation and even including the return to Zion. Never mind the details; hear the intention. This is a heartfelt prayer from the people to their God, a rehearsal of God's past victories so as to plead for present mercies. It marks a change of attitude.

God hears and responds (vv. 12–16). He asserts full authority and offers dramatic reassurance. Mere mortals—even oppressors like Nebuchadnezzar, for example (v. 13)—fade like grass. God can be trusted, because the comfort of the Creator is prior to the fury of any oppressor. Alongside the stretching of the heavens and the founding of the earth was God's hiding of his people in the shadow of his hand.

REFLECTION

Spend a few moments hiding in the shadow of God's hand.

WAKE UP! WAKE UP!

In the previous passage the people urged God to wake up (51:9). In this one, twice God urges his people to wake up (51:17; 52:1). Previously the people urged God to clothe himself with strength (51:9); here God urges Zion to put on their garments of strength (52:1). The poetic reversal is magnificent.

Damsel in distress

Jerusalem is in a bad way. Just like Babylon, called a 'daughter' in chapter 47, Jerusalem is pictured as a woman. She is prostrate on the ground, starving and ruined. Her children have been snared like antelopes in a poacher's net. She is drunk with the cup of God's wrath, and shamed (51:17–20). But this description of Jerusalem is only by way of background, in order to highlight what her deliverance will mean (51:21—52:2). A radical reversal is on the cards. The cup of God's wrath will change hands to her oppressors. As explained in 47:2–3, 'Miss Babylon' will be the one who is shamed: ordered to sit on the ground and to strip. Here, the humiliation of one woman brings the restoration of another—Babylon's downfall will mark Jerusalem's rebirth—even though 52:13 to 53:12 will demonstrate that this correlation is not necessary.

Meanwhile, daughter Jerusalem is given beautiful garments. The feminine imagery of the city continues in 52:1–6, but it now focuses on the healing and holiness of this abandoned woman. God is holy, and now Jerusalem is to reflect his nature and become the holy city, just as described in 4:2–6. The name of God will not be profaned: all who inhabit the holy city will come to know the holy God. Thus those who are uncircumcised and unclean (an expression of disdain referring to those who are enemies of God and those who have oppressed his people) will not be allowed in. The new order is utterly perfect: the holy city and the holy name are identified together. Its inhabitants, though once enslaved and alienated, oppressed and abused, will find total liberation and redemption. That is, they will know God's name and hear his voice.

'Your God reigns'

Chapter 52:7–10 describes what they will hear. First of all comes the beautiful sound of a messenger's feet. The sound is beautiful because the herald brings good news, reasserting the 'gospel' of the age of peace and salvation, as in 40:9. God is returning to Zion, where he will reign—just as Psalm 99 depicts it. In some ways, the repetition feels like a joyful conclusion to Second Isaiah, a return to that exciting but bewildering opening announcement following countless chapters of explanation and reassurance. This passage confirms the same events, bringing their inauguration a little closer. 'In plain sight' the sentinels see the Lord returning to Zion (v. 8). This is the reverse of Ezekiel's vision of God's glory leaving Zion (Ezekiel 8—11), but it is more: it is not just a vision, but a reality that even sentinels observe. It is time for the ruins of Jerusalem to burst into song.

But 52:10 takes the announcement an important stage further than before: not only will Jerusalem break into singing at this comfort and redemption, but all the ends of the earth will see God's salvation. Surely this addresses the final goal of God's plan, extending beyond the strict bounds of God's chosen people Israel. All the nations will observe this rolling up of God's sleeves to bare his holy arm and demonstrate his power. The drama with which Zion embraces salvation will serve as testimony for the whole earth. Everyone will discover how 'your God reigns'. Once again the people are charged to be witnesses (compare 43:10; 44:8).

Since God has called, there is no reason for delay. They are charged to 'Depart!' and 'Go!'—to get up and get on with it (v. 11)! This sounds like another wake-up call. The prophet is urging these despondent people to shift themselves: to get up from Babylon and get on with the journey to Jerusalem. What's more, they are to enjoy the journey as a triumphal procession. They have no need to hide or hurry—unlike in the first exodus. They can be bold—so long as they guard their purity. For Israel is liberated: liberated from panicking about external threats and liberated to celebrate God's own presence. God is returning to Zion, and it seems that he is returning among the people who are called by his name, as their front- and rear-guard.

PRAYER

*Pray for a person or people in need, that they might glimpse how
'your God reigns'.*

The SUFFERING SERVANT (I)

Here is probably the best-known, yet most-contested chapter of Isaiah, if not of the whole Old Testament. Second Isaiah has laid out all things necessary for the restoration of Jerusalem, both city and people, when, without any explanation, the subject returns to the servant, the decisive agent in God's work. This passage consists of a sustained reflection on the servant's calling. It builds on those earlier passages that focused on the servant (42:1–4, 49:1–6; 50:4–9), assuming here the individual figure who functions for Israel as well as on behalf of Israel for the nations. But it develops in particular the aspect of struggle introduced at 49:4 and 50:6. Here, that suffering is seen as integral to the calling: suffering is the means to victory; brokenness is the path to wholeness. Moreover, the suffering is vicarious, for it is the wounds of the servant that make possible healing for others. This idea of vicarious redemptive suffering is totally new: it is found nowhere else in the Old Testament.

The chapter divides into three sections, which we will consider here in turn. First, there is a divine speech (52:13–15); second, a confession from an unnamed 'we' who respond (53:1–11a); and third, another speech from God (53:11b–12).

High and lifted up

Even though the identity of the servant figure is (in any case) a mystery, the servant has become unrecognizable (52:14). We may suppose that the opposition to his teaching has grown since 50:4–9, and smiting and spitting have turned more violent. The nature of the disfigurement is not explicit, but clearly he does not 'look the part' as God's servant. Kings and nations will be shocked and surprised to see him (52:15), not only because of the horror of his appearance, but also because of the height to which he is lifted (52:13).

In the exaltation of this humiliated servant, there are those who come to see and understand, who had not previously heard (compare 48:6–8), even though the Hebrew text does not make clear exactly who 'they' are (52:15b). Even what is seen and understood is not yet explicit: the story of the servant's humiliation begins from 53:2. Yet the echo of 52:13 with 6:1 can be seen to hint at a parallel between this witness to the servant and Isaiah's vision of God.

The testimony of witnesses

The next section, 53:1–11a, is voiced by an unexplained 'we' who testify to an innocent, 'normal' person who became hated, then rejected and mistreated. Given that the 'we' speaks of 'our transgressions' (53:5) and 'my people' (53:8), we take it to be an Israelite confession, even though there has been no evidence for Israelites believing as well as hearing the message of Second Isaiah so far. Perhaps it is a projected response, one which is awaited.

The normal assumption about suffering is that it represents God's punishment for that person's sin, but this servant suffers because of other people's suffering and sin—when, by implication, he did not deserve it. And this suffering brings healing, not simply for him but for all of 'us': 'upon him was the punishment that made us whole, and by his bruises we are healed' (53:4–5). Those speaking here are acknowledging this servant as the key to their restoration and well-being (53:6)—not as if by accident but by the intention of God.

Verses 7–9 affirm that the servant was not only innocent of the sin with which he identified, but he remained willing and silent even when treated unfairly. This servant self-consciously chose this path; yet he was not self-appointed. He was fulfilling God's will (53:10): the servant was serving God, to compensate for the rebellious people who had not served or submitted to God, neither before nor during exile. The confession ends by describing a reversal of fortunes: somehow a transformation takes place, from agony and sin-offering to long life (afterlife?), offspring and knowledge. The second divine speech addresses this transition (53:11b–12).

God's confirmation

The witnesses declared the servant to be the revelation of God's arm (53:1; compare 52:10). Now God declares the servant as the righteous one, whose impact is not just about astonishing or startling many (52:14–15) but about making righteous the many—by bearing their sins (53:11). It is this that explains his exaltation and blessing.

PRAYER

Bring vindication, O Lord, to those who suffer
as a result of others' wrongs.

The SUFFERING SERVANT (II)

It is hard for Christians to imagine how this text might have sounded originally. God's calling of a servant who represents what all Israel is called to be and do is not unusual. The servants whom God chose in the past exemplified, in their own lives, God's intentions for all people. Abraham became the archetypal recipient of blessing, for example, which was a blessing promised to all people. Jacob is even named Israel, because he represents the whole nation yet to be fully formed. Moses' encounter with God at Sinai expresses God's longing to relate closely to all his people. All Israel becomes a servant when it embraces the divine will and plan as demonstrated by the individual servants. But when the people do not obey God's word, then the servant stands over against the people as a rebuke and as an invitation to conversion. This helps to explain the mystery of the servant figure in Second Isaiah. On one hand, the servant represents Israel, and the servant's call expresses what all Israel is called to be and do. On the other hand, when Israel proves unfaithful or disinterested—increasingly through Second Isaiah—the servant is depicted as the chosen, obedient individual whose task is to restore Israel as well as to be a light to the nations.

In the first two servant songs, we can see the servant as representing Israel: in 42:1–4 witnessing to God's supremacy and in 49:1–6 embarking, like Moses, on another exodus-like journey through the wilderness. From 50:4–11, however, he is increasingly cast in the other mode, presenting an uncomfortable challenge to Israel and meeting with opposition even while serving their needs. In 52:13—53:12, this latter mode is especially poignant, given that his suffering at the hands of those he serves ultimately brings about their healing and restoration as well as that of the nations.

Simeon

Even with the hindsight of Jews re-established in the land of Israel with a rebuilt temple, Second Isaiah's message was not complete. Thus, perhaps 600 years after Second Isaiah, at the turning point of the eras in the year 'zero', we find a man described as 'righteous and devout' who is still looking for the consolation of Israel (Luke 2:25).

It turns out that he recognizes God's salvation in the long-promised Messiah at the dedication of a newborn in the temple. Simeon holds the baby called Jesus, and quotes from Isaiah to identify this Messiah also as the servant: 'a light for revelation to the Gentiles and for glory to your people Israel' (Luke 2:32; compare Isaiah 42:6; 49:6). Something was still incomplete with regard to the prophecy of the servant; but Simeon recognizes that it will be completed in Christ. Furthermore, he unites the expectation concerning the future Davidic king with the promise of a suffering servant.

The Ethiopian

Simeon's insight was rare. The story of the Ethiopian in Acts 8:26–40 illustrates that Isaiah 53 was far from clear to many. The Ethiopian articulates the question that niggled Jews for centuries: 'About whom does the prophet say this, about himself or about someone else?' (Acts 8:34). It is clear to him that although Israel was called to be God's servant, Isaiah 53:7–8 relates to some other—an individual. Philip's reply is not a simple one-word answer because, indeed, there is no simple answer. Yet, 'starting with this scripture, he proclaimed to him the good news about Jesus' (Acts 8:35). The suffering servant helps to explain Jesus. That is not to claim that the suffering servant is Jesus—in the manner of prophecy and fulfilment—so much as to point to the model of the servant for an understanding of Jesus. Christians may claim that Jesus is the suffering servant without supposing that the suffering servant is (and only is) Jesus. The servant carried meaning and significance prior to Jesus.

In conclusion, the suffering servant introduces the model for God's redeeming work in the world. According to plan, he works through the concrete particularity of a chosen people—focused, eventually, on a designated person—to bring blessing to all. According to this unique text in the Old Testament, suffering need not be meaningless: it may be purposeful. In particular, through the suffering of God's servant, a pathway to wholeness becomes available, not for the servant himself but vicariously, for others. This notion of a wounded healer is what Christians recognize, writ large, in the death and resurrection of Jesus.

PRAYER

As Jesus to Israel, so the Church to the world. Do you embrace the call to serve, even to suffer?

Moving On

The suffering and cost described in chapter 53 now flower into the healing and abundance described in chapters 54 and 55. First, the feminine imagery of a woman, barren (vv. 1–3) and forsaken (vv. 4–6), expresses the humiliation of exile as well as God's covenant love for Zion. God speaks directly into this pain (vv. 7–10), before the joys of restoration begin to unfurl (vv. 11–17; 55:1–13).

Your tent is too small

Zion's childlessness is underlined three times in 54:1: 'barren... did not bear... have not been in labour'. This makes clear the fruitless-ness of Israel's recent past, yet it serves not so much to describe her dire plight as to contrast how different are the future prospects in God's hands. In Israel's tradition, Sarah is the classic 'barren woman', yet God blessed her and fulfilled his promises to her against all odds (see Genesis 18 and 21). So again, with this barren nation, God is promising blessing. The outcome of the servant's suffering is the nation's prosperity. Children are the practical expression of this future hope. So 'Ms Zion' therefore needs to extend and reinforce her house-hold tents in anticipation—another allusion to the life of Abraham and Sarah. The return from exile may be the opportunity for the ful-filment of God's ancient promises to Abraham, for somehow their descendants will incorporate 'the nations' (v. 3).

In the next verses, Mount Zion is viewed as the forsaken wife, abandoned by her husband in her youth, but now urged to 'move on' (v. 4). Then some familiar language echoes from earlier parts of Second Isaiah (for example, 43:1): 'Do not fear'. She is entreated not to fear, while the register of fears is recited but negated: you will not be ashamed, you will not suffer disgrace, you will not remember the shame of youth and the disgrace of your widowhood. She need not fear, furthermore, for God is her husband and her redeemer (the kinsman who bears the family responsibility for rescuing the relative in need). And, by the way, he is the Creator, the Holy One of Israel and the God of the whole earth (v. 5)! And now he calls her yet again, despite the abandonment (v. 6; compare 43:1). Ultimately, he is not abandoning her.

For a brief moment... but everlasting

There follows a remarkable passage of personal address from God in verses 7–10. You can almost hear the tones of God as lover, crying over his own act of abandonment, acknowledging the agony of anger and renewing his vows of covenant love for his beloved. The tenderness is stirring. Even more remarkable is the candid admission, on God's own lips, that he abandoned Israel in exile. This is not the language of sin and punishment—the exile is not justified—but is an undefended acknowledgment that 'for a brief moment I abandoned you' (v. 7). God also acknowledges a moment of overflowing anger.

Like the previous section, these confessions serve not so much to explore the past as to highlight the future. God expresses his great compassion and everlasting love. He promises an end to anger and rebuke, just as he promised Noah an end to flooding (Genesis 9:11). Moreover, in verse 10, he reasserts his covenant—the covenant that Israel presumed to have ended: 'my steadfast love shall not depart from you, and my covenant of peace shall not be removed'. Like a marriage that has grown stronger after a storm, their future with God benefits from a reinforced covenant. There is less taken for granted, there is more freedom of honesty, and there are renewed expressions of commitment.

Servants of the Lord

What follows in verses 11–17 describes God's lavish rebuilding of Jerusalem, its buildings and its people. The city sparkles with sapphires and rubies, with children taught by God and with 'weapons' of righteousness. These hint at the great vision for Jerusalem outlined in 2:1–4, at least concerning its own people, if not other nations. And in the final verse the people are described as 'servants of YHWH'—the only plural instance of this phrase used in Second Isaiah. The suffering servant was promised posterity: through his labours many would be made righteous (53:10–11). So here God's people are promised posterity, and established in righteousness (vv. 1, 14). Through the individual suffering servant, all come to be designated 'servants of the Lord'.

THINK

We often reflect on how weak we feel without God. But how does God feel when we turn away from him?

COME, SEE

Especially in the wealthy West, we are surrounded by special offers. 'Buy now—pay later'; 'Sale—50% off'; 'Interest-free credit'; and so on. Here in verse 1 is an even better deal. Picture a surprise hawker, calling out in a crowded marketplace, 'Free wine! Free milk!' Will anyone hear and respond?

The invitation

The offer constitutes an enthusiastic invitation to share in God's promised gifts and enter into his abundant joy. 'Everyone who thirsts' is urged to 'come... come, buy and eat... come, buy... listen... eat... delight yourselves... listen' (vv. 1–3). These material benefits are the symbol of spiritual blessings: the purpose is 'that you may live' (v. 3; compare Deuteronomy 8:7–10; 12:15). It is an invitation not just to eat and drink but to feast extravagantly—in other words, to live abundantly. Abundance is the key; in verse 7 God even pardons 'abundantly'.

This new life is made possible through the everlasting covenant, tied to God's steadfast, sure love for David (v. 3). To the exiles this is a painful subject, for God's promise of an everlasting dynasty to David (2 Samuel 7; confirmed in Isaiah 7, 9 and 11) appeared to be broken. His love no longer seemed steadfast or sure. But here the central issue is named and faced, not avoided, in order that healing can happen and new possibilities can grow. In the process, the tradition is redefined.

The promises God made with David are redirected, not to another David, a new king in David's line, but to the Davidic people through whom God always intended to achieve his purposes. Here is another affirmation of the role of God's people in his plans, an underlining of their role as his servant. What God called David to be—witness, leader, commander for the peoples (v. 4)—so God is now calling the people to be (v. 5). Thus, God's promise to David is not a defunct detail of history. It is an ongoing reality for those who continue in their calling as 'servants of YHWH', thanks to their inheritance through the work of the suffering servant (54:17). This calling underlines the call to the nations extended to Israel in 42:6 and continuing (though focused on an individual servant) in 49:6. They are to reflect the glory of God and welcome the nations who respond. So, in the last chapter of Second

Isaiah, the messianic promises of First Isaiah are brought together with the mission of the servant of Second Isaiah, to explain the new world order. This joining of traditions is confirmed in Third Isaiah, where the new age is further explored (chs. 65—66).

Joy and peace?

This calling represents an invitation, not an obligation. Will God's people respond? Will they choose God's free offer of feasting over the daily grind of surviving? And will they seek God rather than sticking to their old wicked ways (vv. 6–7)? Seizing the opportunity of the future that God is offering involves responding to God and relying on God. As we have seen throughout Second Isaiah, Israel in exile has grown resistant, despite God's repeated readiness to pardon (v. 7).

Drawing near to God involves risk. Certainly, God's ways stand in stark contrast to those of Israel in exile (vv. 8–9), and there is no middle ground. God's way may seem surprising—homecoming through Cyrus, for example—but God's plans prevail. This is because of the power of his word, as announced at the outset of Second Isaiah (40:8) and now neatly repeated at the conclusion.

When something goes wrong, a common human reaction is to doubt the power and goodness of God. Despair breeds pessimism, such that even when a solution presents, it is supposed that either God can't do it or he won't do it. But God's word holds supreme. It brings life, as reliably as snow and rain fall (vv. 10–11). Although it brought exile, it will also bring homecoming—when all nature will sing in harmony to Israel's joyful procession (vv. 12–13). Echoing the language of the exodus, they will 'go out' from Babylon with joy and return to Jerusalem in peace, agents of cosmic significance.

Here is Israel's chance to overcome the deafness and blindness that has beset them since Isaiah began (ch. 1). Here they are invited to come (v. 1) and listen (v. 2) and see (vv. 4, 5). It is the same call that echoes to and through the first disciples of Jesus, not least through a Samaritan woman who was offered free water to cure her thirst (John 1:39, 46; 4:29). Will they come and find their cure?

REFLECTION

Like free wine, does this offer seem too good to be true?

OUTSIDERS BECOME INSIDERS

The third section of Isaiah, chapters 56—66, opens with a striking summons to justice and righteousness (vv. 1–2), followed by a reflection on the place of the foreigner within Israel (vv. 3–8). These two themes characterize the remaining chapters of the book. Both relate to the expectation of a divine intervention in the world as part of the continued unfolding of God's plan for his creation set out in both First and Second Isaiah.

Second Isaiah ended with an invitation to play a part in God's intervention, to 'go out (from Babylon) in joy and be led back (home to Jerusalem) in peace' (55:12). It seems that this homecoming has now happened: Third Isaiah is presented from the perspective of a people who are resettling in Jerusalem, renegotiating their lives and priorities. While (we may suppose) there is a historical gap of at least one generation between chapters 55 and 56 (Third Isaiah might be dated around 520BC), yet there is continuity to the story and the message.

Reciprocity

Keeping justice and doing righteousness are urged for the coming of God's salvation (v. 1). Although homecoming has technically taken place, God's promises of salvation are still awaited. But they are not to be awaited in passivity and complacency. God's relationship with Israel is mutual, such that Israel's response to God elicits God's promises towards Israel. In other words, Israel's faithfulness helps to usher in God's salvation.

It is not that Israel's obedience is the requirement and condition for salvation. Israelite faith is too easily presented as a legalistic 'salvation by works', which actually misrepresents the biblical witness. Rather, the covenant relationship between God and his people is reciprocal, as set out from the beginning (Exodus 19:3–6) when the offer of a covenant was first made.

Thus the promises of salvation in Second Isaiah (for example, 40:9–11) must be understood as coupled with the people's faithful response. Whereas Second Isaiah focused on the reality of God's promises, Third Isaiah's concern centres on Israel's response—as if to redress the balance. In fact, this concern represents a return to First Isaiah's emphasis on justice and righteousness (see 1:17, 27; 5:7; 9:7). In First Isaiah, it was expressed in relation to the widow, the orphan and the alien. Third Isaiah explicates faithfulness in terms of keeping sabbath and shunning evil (v. 2) before turning to the issue of foreigners—for whom just the same behaviour is suggested.

Joined to the Lord

Verse 3 takes for granted the presence of foreigners who have become 'joined to the Lord'. This is a remarkable assertion. 'New' Jerusalem is depicted with people from other nationalities, as well as with eunuchs—both contested categories who were previously specifically excluded from temple worship according to Deuteronomy 23:1–8. Clearly they expect to be rejected and excluded—'separated', a term used to counter disorder, confusion and impurity. But eunuchs are to be included, according to three stipulations (v. 4)—keeping sabbath, choosing what pleases God and holding to the covenant—which are precisely the norms for Israel as set out in verse 2. Similarly, verse 6 sets out the expectations for foreigners. These address the intentions of their relationship with God—to minister to him, to love his name and to be his servant—which are just the same priorities as for Israel. It is as if these verses expound Israel's foundational priorities as enshrined in Torah (the law), only now extending them to those who previously were excluded.

The real significance of this full participation, whereby 'imposters' are included in the worship of God at his holy mountain, is not lost for Isaiah. Verse 7 depicts it as a fulfilment of 2:1–4, an underlining of God's ultimate intention that his house will be for all peoples without restriction. It is God who sits at the welcome desk. Homecoming, for him, requires no passport control and no immigration restrictions, only the devoted, joyful offering of prayer and sacrifice. In the aftermath of exile, surely it is clear to Israel—lest anyone should boast—that they were also outcasts, no less than the eunuchs and foreigners (v. 8). God's radical agenda is about ending the exclusion of exile for all.

REFLECTION

Who are the 'eunuchs' and 'foreigners' excluded from your community? Do you dream of seeing them at God's holy mountain?

ABIDING EVIL

The opening chapter of Third Isaiah takes a sharp turn at 56:9, from joyful visions of God's inclusion to threatening declarations of God's judgment. The holy mountain is the place where God will gather all nations (2:2) and be revealed finally and fully (40:9). Yet it is also the place that establishes a sharp distinction between those who worship truly (56:6–7) and those who do not. The latter are described here as hungry dogs and (in modern idiom) 'fat cats' (56:10–11), as adulterers and idolaters (57:3, 13). Chapter 56:9–12 borrows imagery from First Isaiah to describe how Israel's leaders—the sentinels and shepherds—continue to fail their people, acting out of self-interest and for personal gain, and declining to challenge or be challenged. And 57:5 borrows from other early prophets as well, to depict the extent of their depravity: burning with lust among the oaks (compare Hosea 4:12–13; Isaiah 1:29; Jeremiah 3:6), playing the harlot under every green tree (compare Deuteronomy 12:2; Jeremiah 3:6, 13; Ezekiel 6:13), and sacrificing their children (Ezekiel 16:20–21).

Plus ça change?

It is as if nothing has changed. Just as with the wicked and rebellious generation denounced by First Isaiah in the days of Ahaz and Hezekiah, there are still evil elements present within the community. Despite the humiliation of captivity, the lessons of exile and the gift of rescue, they are still seeking their own gain and opposing God's new world. Only the most cynical would not be disappointed.

After exploring some of the exciting, if shocking, universal dimensions to God's plan of salvation in the inclusion of those previously barred from participation in worship (56:1–8), Third Isaiah now turns to those who would undermine it. Despite the present deliverance and the future hope of a new age of God's rule (65:25), the evils of the past continue in the present. There seems to be an abiding evil, casting a shadow even on the rule of God (63:1–6; 66:24). This is the problem confronting Third Isaiah.

In First Isaiah, it was the rebellion of the whole nation—expressed as a hardening, particularly of its leaders—against God. In tension with this aspect of evil and juxtaposed in the very same chapters

(1; 6—9; 11; 12) was an end-time hope of triumph for a faithful remnant, by means of messianic salvation. In Second Isaiah, the relationship between the evil and the good was represented chronologically by the former and the latter things (41:21–22; 42:9). The old age would pass and the new age would dawn, when Israel's captivity in Babylon would end (48:20; 55:12–13). God's promised salvation is enacted in the role of the suffering servant, fulfilling Israel's mission to the world through his obedient suffering and death in atonement.

This simple sequence of the old to the new—even within an end-time expectation of the Messiah or the suffering servant—focuses the problem. Why is there the continuing presence of evil, given the very real experience of deliverance? This is not a psychological problem, about disappointment over the failure of Isaiah's promises to materialize, so much as a theological problem about God's work of restoration.

Third Isaiah's answer—in so far as there is resolution—suggests an ontological rather than chronological relationship between the old and the new. That is, the new has not neatly replaced the old, for the old remains in all its violence and opposition. The two co-exist side-by-side until the coming age is complete. It is not that they cannot be distinguished, for chapter 56 delineates the twin realities very clearly in verses 1–8 and 9–12, and by the end of chapter 66 the fate of the righteous and the wicked is also spelt out. Rather, it seems to be a case of the wheat and the tares (Matthew 13:24–30): both grow together until harvest time.

Whoever takes refuge

In the meantime, there are those who blatantly abuse the language of God's high and lofty mountain. The very place designated for God's true worship for all nations (2:2) has become a focus for false worship and flagrant idolatry (57:7). Not all have turned to their own way, however. Those who take refuge in God are reminded of earlier promises that still stand: they will possess the land and inherit the holy mountain. It is not just the location that marks them out, but their worship.

REFLECTION

*Can you focus on the age to come, despite the setbacks
of the present?*

HE WHOSE NAME IS HOLY

It is common in the Old Testament for a name to denote a nature: thus Jacob means 'he supplants' (Genesis 25:26), Gad means 'fortune' (Genesis 30:11), and Israel means 'the one who strives with God' (Genesis 32:28). Here in verse 15, God's name is described as 'Holy'. The name underlines the quality of holiness as God's most essential nature. This recalls the central vision of the book of Isaiah, of the overwhelming holiness of God that the prophet glimpsed in the temple (ch. 6). The name develops some of the same features, now associated with restoration rather than judgment: God's sovereignty ('the high and lofty one who inhabits eternity') and, chiefly, God's moral purity.

High and holy... contrite and humble

This similarity only adds to the paradox that is depicted: God 'dwells' (in the sense of being enthroned) beside the contrite and the humble. The high and holy place is with the lowly. The contrary position—of pride, haughtiness, self-deception and lack of knowledge—remains the chief obstruction (compare 5:15). The next chapter illustrates this with regard to fasting.

The paradox is paralleled in 66:1–2: although heaven is his throne and the earth his footstool, the place of God's 'rest' is with the one who is humble and contrite in spirit, who trembles at his word. The sentiment suggests that of course God is present in the usual places —in his house, for example—but that is irrelevant compared to the value of his particular presence with those to whom he looks, those who are humble enough to be worthy.

The Christian account of restoration

For Christians reading about the promised restoration in Third Isaiah, it is hard to miss details of correspondence in this picture with the kingdom of God that Jesus inaugurates. Mary's song in Luke 1:46–55 (the Magnificat) depicts a similar paradox whereby God has 'scattered the proud', 'put down the mighty' and 'exalted those of low degree' (Luke 1:51–52, RSV). It is striking, in parallel with verse 15 here, how Mary declares of the Lord, 'Holy is his name.'

In the kingdom of God, it is 'the poor' (Luke 6:20) or 'the poor in spirit' (Matthew 5:3) who are blessed. God is biased towards those who are humble, those who know their need of his healing grace and those who long for salvation.

Prepare the way

In order for the age of restoration to come, it is urged that the people 'build up, prepare the way, remove every obstruction' (v. 14). The images are rather reminiscent of building a motorway, just as in 40:3–5. The matter of pride remains the chief obstruction to the fulfilment of God's purposes and plan. Yet despite their pride, there remains for the people of God a role within God's plan. By their response to God, they play a part in determining when and how God will act. They are the ones who are responsible for preparing the road by which God's restoration will arrive.

Nevertheless, whether people respond or not, God promises to act definitively. 'For I will not contend for ever, nor will I always be angry' (v. 16, RSV). They have the opportunity to participate in God's plan or to exclude themselves from it. For some, this will consist of real healing and real peace. For others, there will be no peace (vv. 18–21). God has given his people the free will to choose for themselves.

This passage acts rather like an evangelistic sermon, presenting 'two ways to live'. It urges the people to choose humility, peace and healing over pride, selfishness and restlessness. Although they have chosen wrongly in the past, they still have the opportunity to choose again.

REFLECTION

What are the obstacles to the high and lofty God making his dwelling with you?

SEEKING GOD

Recalling chapter 40, God commissions someone to make another announcement, to shout (as in 40:6) and lift up the voice (as in 40:9). But this time the megaphone is to tell the world of something shameful: his people's rebellion and sin. Even though they are supposedly seeking God (just as 55:6 requested), something is wrong in their lives. Perhaps the biggest problem is that they don't realize it. All they realize is that God isn't answering their prayers (v. 3).

Blind spots

The problem of unanswered prayer is a difficult one: it is not the focus of concern here, but one symptom of a bigger issue. The issue concerns the people's blindness. They are unaware of their sin and rebellion. They continue in their daily lives blissfully and blithely. They think of themselves as devout, disciplined and delighting in God, but our self-image can be wholly mistaken. The fundamentals are out of sync: somehow their perspective is distorted. Rather like the preacher who does not practise what he or she preaches, so here the people ask about righteousness and justice, yet don't practise it (v. 2). On the one hand they seek God, while on the other hand they seek their own interests. There is a clash, but they don't know it. Self-awareness has turned to self-deception: basic matters of integrity are at stake.

Individually, in situations like this, we need a friend to point to the plank that we might not otherwise recognize in our own eye (compare Matthew 7:3–5). Here it is the whole community that is blind. So, for example, they take pride in their humility; they fast, yet at the same time serve their own whims; they oppress their workers while they supposedly seek justice (v. 3). This is not so much hypocrisy as ignorance. They are not insincere, but keenly committed. They pat each other on the back to spur one another on, not realizing the gaping omissions and mistakes that they share. What they need is fresh insight—a discerning mentor or (as here) a courageous prophet —to help them distinguish between the wood and the trees, to help them see their failings, to help them bring their personal practice of piety into line with its corporate social dimensions.

The point of fasting

The focus moves to the practice of fasting in particular (vv. 6–7). It is too easy to focus on the inward side—the personal disciplines and sacrifices related to food—and ignore the outward aspects relating to others, especially those for whom such choices would be a luxury. Generosity is a spiritual discipline as much as abstinence. Fasting—forgoing food and possessions—should benefit all God's people. And God's justice for all his people demands particular attention to the poor and hungry, the homeless and the helpless. The concern focuses on economic justice and social inclusion, and the practice of fasting is singled out—perhaps because it leads so readily to false humility.

In the previous section, the high and lofty God announced that he dwells with the lowly and humble (57:15). And the premise of chapter 58 is that when God is sought properly and followed wholly —when humility is genuine—he makes himself fully known (vv. 8–14). This is no reluctant concession when certain conditions are met. It is the dazzling transformation of darkness as the day dawns. It is the surprising turn from hopelessness to healing, from despair to glory, from desolation to restoration. Nevertheless, there is a priority to be noted. We experience God most fully when we feed the hungry and welcome the homeless (compare also Matthew 25:34–45). And we usher in God's dawn—we participate in bringing in God's kingdom—when we ourselves work for justice and healing in his world. In verses 13–14 this issue is focused on keeping the sabbath: the weekly reminder of what matters most.

'Here I am'

God's presence is expressed most fully by the response to his people's call. Previously it was God who called and Isaiah who responded, saying 'Here I am' (6:8). Now God leaps to attention with the same enthusiasm and with the exact same expression to his servants: 'Here I am' (v. 9). God longs to be at his people's service, fully and freely. No one can complain that he does not hear prayer, for he does not hold back. Just like Isaiah, when God is called, he responds.

REFLECTION

If you were ever prone to false humility, who would let you know?
Do you listen to them often enough?

SIN, REPENTANCE & ASSURANCE

'Has anything changed with God's people?' we may wonder yet again. This chapter of judgment is, in many ways, reminiscent of First Isaiah. The people are reprimanded for their sin and reminded of its consequences. It comes as a shock. Have they learnt nothing from the experience of exile? Maybe just one thing: how to charge God when he seems slow to save. They presume that it is God's fault. Like some of the disputations in Second Isaiah (for example, ch. 50), this chapter begins by refuting the accusation. God's power is in no way diminished: his hand is not too short to save, or his ear too dull to hear (v. 1). The problem does not lie with God.

The theological nature of sin and evil

The problem lies with the recurrent sinfulness of God's people (vv. 2–8). The focus is not so much on pinpointing particular areas where the people have trespassed, as on grasping the general effect of their pattern of behaviour. Rather than claiming their identity as God's, they continue to cut themselves off from him. By their sinfulness they are distanced from God's righteousness: their sin is described as a barrier (v. 2; compare 50:1–2). As the last chapter also put it (58:4), because of their sin their prayers are not effective.

The language of separation echoes a characteristic 'priestly' understanding of holiness, whereby holy things and clean things are to be distinguished and separated from the unholy and unclean according to a fixed scheme (compare Leviticus 10:10; 20:25). Only now, this system is tragically reapplied to the separation between the holy God and his sinful people. Here is a theological analysis of the effect of sin, one that is taken up by Paul in Romans 3:15–17 to underline how the whole of humanity is dominated by sin. The vivid metaphors that follow expand on this universal dimension. Evil hatches its brood like poisonous vipers (v. 5). It multiplies in an unbroken line of twisted paths, none of which ever lead to peace (v. 8).

What is to be done? How should the faithful few respond in a situation of gross apostasy? And what does God do when justice seems lost and truth abandoned?

A model for confession

In verses 9–15a we hear the voice of faithful Israel. Complaint turns into confession at verse 12, acknowledging the whole nation's wickedness. Those who repent do not offer mitigating excuses: there is no pleading of special circumstances concerning their complicity. The remnant identifies with the entire nation's evil and thus with God's condemnation. They freely confess their guilt and its impact in undermining their relationship to God.

God responds. First he intervenes to establish righteousness, avenging the wicked and redeeming the faithful (vv. 15b–17). This is described in the past tense, affirming that God has not been inactive in Israel up to this point. God's judgment does not relate to one moment in history. It is an ongoing situation, an expression of his will to tackle all forms of evil. This nature is underlined by the enduring picture of God in armour: *he* wears the breastplate of righteousness, the helmet of salvation, the clothes of vengeance (precisely the armour we are told to put on in Ephesians 6:10–17). God engages in the battle.

A promise follows (vv. 18–20). God will bring justice—requital for the perpetrators and acquittal for the sufferers—and he will finally come as redeemer for all who repent, appearing in glory at Zion. Chapters 60—62 relate this glorious hope to the realities of life within the restored city of Jerusalem.

Mind the gap

There remains a gap, a period before the final fulfilment of God's promises. In the last verse, usually regarded as a late addition to the chapter, as if to provide a summary comment, God himself speaks and recalls the covenant as his expression of faithfulness until that final day. Covenant describes the relationship through which God's will has been and continues to be expressed. It is also the means by which those who join themselves to God (56:6) are to be sustained. Subsequent generations are urged to remember, and recall continually, that God has already given them everything they need to follow him.

REFLECTION

What do you complain about? Can you pause, and instead turn the complaint to confession?

GATHERING *for* GLORY

We begin the great central section of Third Isaiah (60—62): a mountain-top of hope and joy and good news concerning the future, compared to the more qualified and complex surrounding material (chs. 56—59; 63—66). It opens with God exhorting the people, in the second person feminine form, to 'Arise, shine!' Instantly this resonates with earlier themes, transforming and reversing the negatives to positives. Previously the city was described in terms of a woman downtrodden and humiliated; now, as promised, she is transformed and exalted (51:17; 60:14). Previously the land was covered in deep darkness; now there is a new dawn (9:2; 60:1–2). Previously the people were scattered; now they are regathered (6:12; 60:4). More generally, the chapter expands on those earlier promises in which the scattered exiles would be brought home in the arms of foreign rulers (49:18, 22–23).

Power in submission

The nations have a place in this great homecoming. In 2:1–4 the motivation behind the vision was theological: from the nations' perspective, they migrated to God's holy mountain so as to learn his ways. Here the movement is described from the Israelite perspective, compounded by its political and economic import. Gigantic camel caravans are envisaged, crossing the desert and converging on Jerusalem, bringing their finest produce of precious goods and livestock. Although these gifts are brought in praise of God (vv. 6, 9), their political significance is not missed. What is given in worshipful submission to God is also interpreted as political submission to Jerusalem. Whereas for centuries Israel had been paying tribute to various other imperial powers—Assyria, Babylon, Persia—now the direction of servitude is reversed. Matthew 2:11 alludes to the same glorious subversion (compare Isaiah 60:6). The (Gentile) 'wise men from the east' are described as bringing to the baby Jesus gold and frankincense—symbols of worship and a means of acknowledging his messianic identity while simultaneously challenging the power of Herod.

There is little doubt that Zion's future magnificence is seen to involve an accumulation of material splendour. Some have read this as crude post-exilic nationalism: a consumer-based vision of success whereby the nations' self-giving becomes Israel's profit, and the nations' self-offering becomes Israel's free labour (vv. 10, 14). The attitude seems a far cry from the humility encouraged in chapters 57—58, or of him who 'emptied himself, taking the form of a servant' (Philippians 2:7, RSV).

Verses 10–16 pursue in further detail the reversal of Zion's fortunes. There are foreigners to rebuild walls, superfluous kings to minister, and various kinds of luxurious timber freely available for construction, yet the focus is not on the material things themselves. The city's gates should remain open, even at night, suggesting that there is no need to defend this wealth. Rather, the place must be open and welcoming to further streams of pilgrims (v. 11). What matters is not so much the beauty and majesty of the city itself as the fact that it is recognized as 'the city of YHWH, the Zion of the Holy One of Israel' and that it bears his marks of peace, righteousness, salvation and praise (vv. 14, 17–18). The character of this city will be totally different from anything known before, so long as people seek the God of mercy who underpins it rather than settling for a superficial appreciation of its material benefits.

God the glory of Zion

The vision of ultimate restoration is focused on God—not on any human contribution to restoration, not on any history that qualifies Zion for renovation, but only on the Creator who holds the power to make all things new. The vision of God's future glory is building ever stronger and brighter as the book of Isaiah leans to its conclusion (vv. 19–22). The city is portrayed in terms of light, just as the original mission of the servant was described as a light to the nations (42:6; 49:6). The sun and moon are replaced by the perpetual shining of God. He is the source and guarantor of Israel and the nations; with him there is no darkness, no night, no mourning and no danger (compare Revelation 22:5). God makes an unqualified promise of total provision—righteousness, land, growth, glory—leading to a final summit announcement (echoing his revelation in a moment of Moses' doubt, Exodus 3:15): 'I am YHWH'.

PRAYER

Lord, you are my everlasting light. Shine on!

TRANSFORMATION

When Jesus started reading this chapter in the synagogue at Nazareth (Luke 4:16–19), he startled the congregation because he claimed this vision of transformation as a manifesto about himself. Previously, the 'I' voice that speaks in this chapter (except in verses 8–9, where God is speaking) had been a source of mystery and speculation. Is this the voice of the prophet, a personal statement concerning God's call in parallel to chapter 6? Or is it a further 'servant song', a continuation of the task of the ambiguous servant figure, whether that be a chosen individual or the collective body of Israel? Whoever performs it, what is clear is that God has a mission for practical transformation.

God's mission

The tasks assigned to this figure correspond in great detail with earlier parts of Isaiah. God's dramatic announcement of comfort— a word that resounds through Second Isaiah—is repeated here, embodied in the phrase 'comfort all who mourn' (v. 2; compare 40:1–2). To bring 'good news to the oppressed', similarly, relates to the mantle of the herald who first announced the good news that God would return in power (v. 1; compare 40:9). In Second Isaiah the role of herald converged with that of the servant (42:1; 48:16), so it comes as no surprise to find the figure in chapter 61 relating the good news to the servant's task of proclaiming liberty to captives and release to prisoners (v. 1; compare 42:7; 49:9). The assurance that 'the spirit of God is upon me' also relates to the servant, though this is less surprising given the expectation that the spirit of God will be upon the offspring of the servant (44:2–3; 54:17). The figure's anointing by the spirit is sometimes also linked with messianic elements of First Isaiah, specifically the promise that 'the spirit of the Lord shall rest on him' (11:2). Thus, in claiming this vision for himself, Jesus was hinting at his identity as fulfilling both roles of Servant and Messiah (Luke 4:21–22).

This mission furthers the expectation from the previous chapter that God is going to reverse the fortunes of Jerusalem. A time of abundance and prosperity is coming, and the description of liberty, favour, gladness and glory further fires the imagination to anticipate that great day. The initial description of transformation—bringing, binding, proclaiming, releasing—culminates in a reference to the practice of jubilees, 'the year of the Lord's favour' (v. 2; compare Leviticus 25:10–55). This related primarily to economic restoration, when all property lost in business transactions was to be restored and returned, reflecting a radical reordering of relationships in society. Such news is certainly good news to the poor, though it may come as bad news to the rich. No wonder that a group rose up to kill Jesus when he proclaimed this text at Nazareth (Luke 4:28–29)! God's mission is undoubtedly directed to those who are weak, powerless or marginalized: the good news involves radical economic restoration. The disadvantaged can thus function fully and joyfully within the community again, a community now depicted with energy and resolve. Like sturdy oak trees (v. 3: revitalized since the withering oak of 1:30), these people now have the capacity to rebuild the ruins of Jerusalem (v. 4). God's spirit is initiating a domino chain of renewal: from freedom and comfort, to financial and social reordering, to urban regeneration and international cooperation (vv. 1–6).

God serves his people through his people. Notice how God is enacting his restoration by, first of all, anointing a particular person. Again and again in Isaiah we have noted God executing his plans through mortals: the Israelite king, the promised Messiah, the foreign powers of Assyria and Babylon, the herald, the servant, and now the figure whose voice is heard in chapter 61. God's will and human vocation are intimately connected.

To God be the glory

God is no one's debtor. Those who have suffered will be rewarded (v. 7). The 'double portion' expresses abundance, referring back to 40:2. When God speaks up at verses 8–9, we glimpse again how generous is his sense of justice: he is far from grudging in his recompense. Israel will luxuriate in blessing, and the nations will know it.

Will the nations see Israel's prosperity—or will they see God's glory? This depends on Israel's attitude (v. 10), and on the fruits of righteousness and praise that it produces (v. 11).

REFLECTION

Try reading 61:1–3 as Jesus did, recognizing the prophecy as commissioning you to join in God's work of transformation.

A CITY NOT FORSAKEN

This chapter begins and ends with Zion-Jerusalem undergoing a name change (vv. 2, 12). At least six new names are voiced—'My Delight Is in Her', 'Married', 'The Holy People', 'The Redeemed of the Lord', 'Sought Out' and 'A City Not Forsaken' (vv. 4, 12)—all of which speak of the relationship of the city and its people to God. This is the defining issue for the life of Jerusalem, the most basic lesson to learn and never again forget. The people exist because of God. Their life can begin again because of God. It is God's unfailing commitment to them, evident in their recent reconciliation and restoration, that permits life to go on. They are no longer abandoned by God (compare 54:7–8), and here, repeatedly, is the poetic expression of that reality. He delights in them, he seeks them, he does not forsake them… he redeems them. They are a crown of beauty and a royal diadem in his hand (v. 3). God rejoices over them (v. 5).

Just as Second Isaiah reassured the Israelites repeatedly that God had not forgotten them and they had no need to fear (see especially comments on chapters 41 and 43, pp. 130–133, 136–139), so here Third Isaiah reminds them again and again how he has loved them and continues to be with them now that they have returned. Essentially the message is the same—'God is with you'—even though these precise words are not used here. Apparently, it does not sink in easily and bears repeating and receiving again and again. God is *with* you: he is not against you (v. 8). God is with *you*: it is you he has chosen—'married'—and redeemed (v. 4). *God* is with you: he who proclaims salvation to the ends of the earth—YHWH, the Lord—is with you (v. 11).

Restlessness

Despite these assurances that they are no longer abandoned by God, there is the suggestion that the people still feel abandoned. Chapters 60—62 have been full of God's promises to restore Jerusalem—'in its time I will accomplish it quickly' (60:22)—but where is the speed and when is the time?

The prophet's reaction to this situation is salutary. The prophet will not keep silent concerning Zion's vindication and Jerusalem's salvation (v. 1). He remains convinced that God will act. Rather than becoming resigned or disillusioned in the absence of fulfilment, he confronts it. This chapter not only reminds the people of God's promises: it also reminds God to act on them. The prophet, in effect, is interceding on behalf of Zion-Jerusalem. Here is an example of persistence in prayer.

The prayer insists that God should not keep silent. Like the judge who is worn down by the widow's persistence (Luke 18:1–8), God will have to answer if he is to get any rest. The prophet has appointed sentinels—watchers—to remind God continually, day and night, until Jerusalem is restored and renowned throughout the earth (vv. 6–7). They will not let God off the hook! Meanwhile, following the logic of such prayer, God will know how eager are his people to receive his intervention.

Prepare the way!

In 40:3–5, the exiled people were commissioned to prepare the way for God to come, to build a highway for his return through the desert to Jerusalem. Here in verse 10, the same command is repeated, yet redirected. This time the highway is explicitly for the people. Whereas in Second Isaiah the emphasis was on freeing the deportees, now it has widened to recognize the presence of the nations also. The city must be ready to receive all peoples, according to the vision at the outset of Isaiah (2:1–4). In case such a broad, inclusive vision threatens the people who still feel themselves abandoned, there is further reassurance regarding their place among the nations. Their produce will not be usurped (v. 8; compare 65:21–22) as all the earth is drawn to God's salvation (vv. 10–11).

PRAYER

Pray for someone in need:
*God is **with** you. God is with **you**. **God** is with you.*

GOD'S VENGEANCE

We may feel tempted to pass over these six verses quickly. They focus on the subject of God's judgment, expressed in a shocking combination of celebratory splendour and terrifying wrath. We focus here not only on the matter of judgment but also on the issues that such uncomfortable material raises for the interpretation of scripture as God's word.

Mighty to save—and judge

Chapters 60 to 62 have focused on God's promise of salvation. The coming of God's redemption is accompanied—indeed, bracketed—by reference to his judgment (59:15–20 and 63:1–6). Vindication and judgment belong together (v. 4). God's establishment of a just and peaceful rule on earth involves him first in acting decisively to right the wrongs of an abusive world. On this basis, God's arrival is anticipated with eagerness. He is the mighty judge, whose justice will bring vindication (literally 'righteousness') and salvation (v. 1; compare 56:1; 61:10; 62:2). They see a warrior coming from the south and, as if at a border-control cross-examination, they ask, 'Who is this?' (v. 1) and 'Why are your robes red?' (v. 2). The Hebrew suggests poetic word-plays between Edom and 'red' (*adom*) and between Bozrah and gathering grapes (*bsr*).

God answers their questions. Note that he is identified by his power to save (not to judge). Yet he explains his red appearance in terms of treading the winepress among the peoples. The metaphor shifts: the red is not juice but blood; and the trampling does not involve grapes, but peoples. Suddenly we realize that the slaughter of Edom and Bozrah, previously foretold in 34:6–7, is here being described as completed action. The grammatical tenses of the verbs in verse 3 also allow this 'day of vengeance' to be extended into the future, suggesting apocalyptic overtones as well as past events. As discussed concerning chapter 34 (pp. 112–113), the particular focus on Edom may be taken to represent God's universal judgment against all peoples.

God's anger is exacerbated by his functioning alone. He looked but found that 'no one was with me' (v. 3) and 'there was no helper'

(v. 5). Elsewhere in Isaiah we have observed how God uses human agents to bring about his work: consider, for example, the call of the prophet Isaiah in speaking for God (6:1–13), and the role of Cyrus in delivering Israel from exile (44:24—45:7). But this is not the case when it comes to standing for justice and siding with God's righteous cause. In 59:16, no one from Israel would stand with him; now there is no one from the nations either. When it comes to judgment, God is found to act alone—here, by necessity more than choice (compare John 12:44–50).

Handling God's bloodstained rage

The divine warrior imagery is shocking. God is depicted trampling and crushing peoples, spattering blood and pouring out life—activity motivated by anger and wrath (vv. 3, 5–6). Such violent language fulfils a common stereotype about the God of the Old Testament. Moreover, it is as if this warrior-God is being celebrated and his fearful judgment recounted as a victory hymn (v. 1). Indeed, the 'Battle Hymn of the Republic' borrows from these lines (and from Revelation 19:15) as it vigorously declares him 'trampling out the vintage where the grapes of wrath are stored'. Can such sentiments be echoed lightly?

These verses are often taken as the extreme expression of a beleaguered people, a declaration of hope by those under threat. As, for example, with Psalm 137, perhaps this is no polished piece, and thus no final word from which to extract a comprehensive understanding of God's judgment, let alone God's nature. Rather, it represents an outlet for frustration whose very passion allows for a renewal of trust amid injustice and suffering. Precisely because this is not representative of the full picture of God in Isaiah, it speaks of Israel's dire straits as much as it speaks of God's activity. Yet, we must acknowledge, these verses belong to scripture: they form a part of God's word to his people. The message of a universal judgment ahead—prior to the vindication and salvation of the faithful—is clear. Meanwhile, we would be wise not to ignore the reality of divine anger, which boils against injustice of all kinds, as seen when Jesus visited the temple (Matthew 21:12–13).

REFLECTION

Do you look forward to God's day of judgment, or do you dread it?
Is it good news or bad? Reflect on what this reveals
about your own life.

A PSALM *of* LAMENT

There is a change of voice at 63:7. Whereas God was the 'I' responding to Israel's questions in 63:1–6, now the voice is that of corporate
Israel, communally reciting God's mercies in the past (63:7–14),
confessing their sin in the present (64:5–7) and pleading for God's
help in the future (63:15—64:12). These are the typical features of
lament psalms (for example, Psalms 44 and 89). The elements also fit
the context of Third Isaiah. Faithful Israel is aware of its own failings
(59:1–15) and the coming judgment (59:15–18; 63:1–6) while also
yearning for the salvation promised to all who fear the name of the
Lord, including even foreigners (59:19–20; compare 56:3–8).

God's fatherly love for Israel

In remembering days of old, the contrast is drawn between the times
of God's favour and the times of his judgment. Constantly it turns
out to be God who remembers Israel, not vice versa. He does so
because of his mercy and his love (63:7, 9). This is seen most
expressly in the events of the exodus (63:11). Just as in the established prayers or 'collects' of some churches, intercession begins with
recalling God's mercy and love in the past. God is summoned—
indeed, persuaded with logical argument—to intervene again, on the
basis of precedent. 'As you have done before, so then, do it again!'
Thereafter, from 63:15, appeal is made—passionately, urgently—to
God's yearning heart, to his fatherly responsibilities and to his sovereign call (63:15, 16, 18–19).

The language found here for God as Father, so easily taken for
granted by those who know the Lord's Prayer, is unusual in the Old
Testament, and is thought to represent a post-exilic development. If
God has claimed his people as sons and daughters (for example, 1:2;
9:6; 43:6), then it is now time for them to realize that they can call
upon him as 'Father'. Despite being children who have previously
frustrated their father's expectations of them, they turn to depend
upon the relationship. As children indeed, they blame him for their
stray wanderings and even presume to tell him how to act (63:17).
Such prayer seems outrageous, but here is honest, direct, real conversation, even if it may not be entirely factually or theologically

correct. In the process, God's sovereignty is acknowledged—it is as if everything depends on him, not them—and they identify themselves as 'servants', 'tribes of your heritage' and God's 'holy people' (63:17–18). In other words, they understand God better; and correspondingly they understand themselves better, as belonging to him.

'Tear open the heavens!'

Chapter 64:1–4 expresses the longing for God to come again, as in the exodus. How often has that sentiment been echoed—not just for God to look (as in 63:15) but actually to intervene and 'do something!' The hope is voiced rather hopelessly. There is irony too, for the words echo God's words at 48:18, 'O that you had paid attention to my commandments!' They did not; so he has not. And so they confess their sins (64:5–7).

It is at this point that they offer themselves afresh to their Father: 'we are the clay, and you are our potter' (64:8). Reworking earlier themes from both First and Second Isaiah, they acknowledge their helplessness as creatures separated from their Creator (29:16; 45:9). Clay, by itself, is useless. The potter needs to claim the clay and shape the pot, if it is to be useful again.

The clay nevertheless petitions the potter to move beyond anger and act according to his steadfast love (64:9). How can he hold himself back (64:12), given the pitiful (exaggerated) state of Jerusalem described in verses 10–11?

'O that you would tear open the heavens and come down,' comes the cry. The heavens are rent open and the new exodus does come—when Jesus is baptized (Mark 1:9–11).

REFLECTION

Are you outrageous in your praying? Do you dare to tell God how to act on the basis of past experience with him?

You Did Not Answer

Previously, the people complained that they called but God did not respond (58:3). Now we discover God calling, but the people failing to respond (vv. 1, 12, 24; 66:4). The final two chapters offer no comfortable ending to the book of Isaiah. Both chapters are structurally complicated: it is hard even to identify their literary subdivisions. Yet both resonate with repeated themes from earlier in the book as well as developing a clear demarcation between the faithful and the unfaithful. Here in verses 1–16 God addresses both groups: firstly apostate Jews in verses 1–7 and secondly the 'servants' in verses 8–16. If this is a response to Israel's lament in the previous section, then God is far from silent, even if his answer to their lament is both challenging and thrilling.

Smoke

There are no accessibility issues when it comes to approaching God. God's call is continuous and his hands remain outstretched, just as Jesus describes the father of the prodigal (vv. 1–2; compare Luke 15: 11–32). God is keen to be found by those who seek him (as also in 51:1; 58:2). He simply waits to be sought, yet he is pained with the awareness of how low his children can go. Verses 2–5 present a catalogue of forbidden practices, illicit cultic activities that threaten the purity of Israel's worship—like smoke in God's nostrils! Those who engage in such activity are judged in the conventional fashion (vv. 6–7; compare Ezekiel 20:28).

Servants

In sharp contrast are God's 'servants' (an expression stressed seven times in vv. 8–9, 13–15), who are those who have sought God (v. 10). They have a glorious future. First this is described in terms of the material blessings of eating, drinking and rejoicing—unlike the hunger, thirst and crying that will afflict those who did not respond to God's invitation (vv. 13–14). As in the beatitudes of Luke 6:20–26, the blessings and curses represent direct opposites. The names of those 'cursed' will become a curse, while those who respond will be given a new name (v. 15; compare 56:5; 62:2). And they will be a blessing: that is, they will bless others by the God of faithfulness, exactly as God first promised to Abraham about his descendants (Genesis 12:3). But note: these 'servants' are no longer ethnically defined. They are those who seek God (vv. 1, 10, 12, 24), including foreigners (56:3–8).

New heavens, new earth

Second Isaiah stressed God as Creator who sustains his initial creation and promises new things (42:5–6; 48:6). Now, it is unveiled that God will create afresh: a new world order radically different from what has gone before. God's faithful people will experience the entry of God's rule within a transformed Jerusalem (vv. 19–23). Whereas previously there were many sorrows, there will be abundant joy. Whereas previously there was premature death, there will be long life. Whereas previously houses were destroyed, new homes will be built. Whereas previously vineyards were wasted, new vines will bear fruit. Whereas previously work was frustrating, in future it will be fulfilling. All that characterized the broken relationship between humanity and God will be healed. These blessings will pass from one generation to the next. And God's accessibility will be such that 'before they call I will answer'! (v. 24).

The final detail about this new creation picks up lines directly from the messianic vision of chapter 11 concerning the wolf and the lamb, and the lion and the ox, on God's holy mountain (v. 25; compare 11:6–9). Even though the point is a controversial one among scholars, it is hard to ignore how this cross-reference might be seen to function in the book of Isaiah. The portrayal of God's new and ultimate world order is allied to—indeed, it is identified with—the age ushered in by the promised Messiah. The messianic promises of First Isaiah, echoed in Second Isaiah in the promise of 'an everlasting covenant, my steadfast, sure love for David' (55:3), now find their place in Third Isaiah, as God's future final promises for the whole of creation are more fully revealed.

REFLECTION

Do you think of prayer as calling to God or responding to God?

FIRE & GLORY

Some people find this final chapter disjointed. Rather we may see, by way of conclusion, a number of strands that have run through Isaiah as a whole coming together.

When I called, no one answered

There is a challenge to those concerned with building a temple. God cannot be contained or controlled: he is sovereign over all creation. Yet, as affirmed in chapter 65, he is fully accessible to the humble, faithful and contrite (vv. 1–2; compare 65:1, 12, 24). There are those who displease him by their worship: those who act as if religious activity alone appeases the Almighty, without responding to God when he calls (vv. 3–4). God's city is thus a place of conflict, resolved only by the heavenly judgment of God (vv. 5–6). This picture differs little from the situation of temple and judgment described in chapter 6.

Giving birth, bringing comfort

The promise of God to his faithful people stands in stark contrast (vv. 7–14), as starkly as the difference between 'servants' and 'enemies' (v. 14). Like a woman giving birth before her labour, God has done the unexpected in bringing to birth the children of Zion. Now their joy exceeds whatever grief existed previously. The promise of comfort (40:1; 49:13) is fulfilled in the image of suckling children at their mother's breast. These children are God's servants: they stand in the path of the servant (50:4–9; 52:13—53:12) and, unlike God's enemies, they stand to claim his inheritance (54:17; 56:6).

The coming of God

Just as promised at 40:10 and 62:11, God is coming in awesome power. He comes with the fire of judgment as well as with the glory of salvation (vv. 15–17, 18–21; compare 63:1–6). As before, the judgment is focused on those who strive to purify themselves falsely by means of pagan rites (v. 17; compare 65:3–5). And this takes place in the gardens, corresponding to 1:28–29.

With regard to the glory, verses 18–23 summarize the eschatological hopes that have accumulated throughout the book. First of all, there is the gathering of all nations from afar (2:2–3; 41:5). They come and they see God's glory (6:1, 3; 40:5). Those who survive (6:5) are then sent as witnesses to declare God's glory among the nations. When the disparate caravans regroup at God's holy mountain—imagine a festival on a mammoth scale—even foreigners are among those chosen to be God's priests (56:6). Finally, the radical vision of God's new heaven and new earth is repeated (65:17–18), as if this is the goal of the earlier promises and the context within which his descendants will worship him for ever (vv. 22–23).

We might want the book to end here, but it does not (even though it may have done at one time). Rather, the division between the faithful and the unfaithful is maintained even at the end times. In spite of all nations worshipping at God's holy mountain—in spite of the new heavens and the new earth—there remain those outside the realm of God's salvation. The book of Revelation cites the same paradox. At the new creation of heaven and earth, God will wipe away every tear (Revelation 21:1–4; compare Isaiah 25:8; 65:17). Yet outside there will be murderers, idolaters and those who practise falsehood (Revelation 22:15). Rather than choosing to see God's glory, alas, they chose to rebel (v. 24).

Standing back

The 'new heavens and new earth' promised at the conclusion of Third Isaiah brings the reader to look back through First and Second Isaiah with new eyes. God's promised deliverance from Babylon, with which Second Isaiah was preoccupied, may now be understood as one instance of God's final purposes for his people. Similarly, God's promised Messiah, an important feature of the early chapters of First Isaiah (chs. 7; 9; 11), may now be viewed within the wider eschatological frame. The messianic imagery borrowed to describe the new creation (65:25) suggests that Zion, transformed and under messianic rule, is integral to God's final overarching goal for his world. The role of the future Messiah and the work of the Suffering Servant need not be distinct as God works out his plan of judgment and salvation.

REFLECTION

Isaiah saw God's glory. The nations will see God's glory.
Have you seen it?

GLOSSARY

In accordance with the purpose of this series, technical terms have been kept to a minimum. Where they do occur, at least for the first time, they are usually explained. The important ones are collected together here for ease of reference.

Ahaz: King of Judah 734–715BC, during the period of the war with Syria and Ephraim (Israel).

Cult: The system given to the people of Israel with which to worship God. It is associated with priests and sacrifice in the temple.

Day of YHWH (the Lord): This is the day when God's original and final purposes will come about. The phrase can be used in Isaiah to refer to the day of judgment, but beyond the judgment it is also used to anticipate the glorious 'day' when God will reign in just judgment and a son of David will reign in just judgment (see Isaiah 16:4–5).

Ephraim/Samaria: Differing names used to describe the northern kingdom, Israel.

Eschatology: The study of the end (Greek: *eschaton*) of everything. Thus 'eschatological' may variously refer to any of the events or times relating to death, judgment, heaven and hell, and eternal life.

Hezekiah: King of Judah 715–697BC. He followed Ahaz and was commonly seen as a good king who raised hopes and brought religious reformation. Assyria invaded Judah under Sennacherib in 701, but Jerusalem was saved.

Isaiah: This name can refer to the book or to the prophet(s) behind it. It should not be taken necessarily to refer to a single eighth-century prophet, as if there was only one 'Isaiah' who authored the book that bears this name. The terms 'First', 'Second' and 'Third' Isaiah relate to the three sections of the book, chapters 1—39, 40—55 and 56—66 respectively. Sometimes they also refer to the author of the section, though this is not intended to assume multiple authorship either.

Israel: This name carries different senses, depending on the period to which it refers. Originally, it refers to the people with whom

God made a covenant at Sinai. Geographically, it is also used to describe the promised land (previously Canaan) in which they dwell. Later, after the reign of Solomon, it comes to be used of one portion of God's people, those who (post-division) live in the northern kingdom. After this kingdom falls in 722BC, it is used once again to refer to God's chosen people, wherever they live, and the land to which they are restored following exile, around 539BC. This latter meaning is the usual one in Isaiah, except for the early chapters (1—23) when it refers to the northern kingdom (often in contrast to its southern counterpart, Judah).

Jerusalem: The capital city of Judah. The name is often used symbolically, as the heart of Judah and Israel, and the place where God reigns in Zion.

Jotham: Followed Uzziah as king of Judah, 741–734BC. The Assyrian empire began to grow during this time.

Judah: The southern kingdom, which included Jerusalem as capital city. This term is used to distinguish the southern kingdom from the northern kingdom of Israel, after they divided around 932BC.

Manasseh: King of Judah 697–642BC. Commonly portrayed as a 'bad' king, who followed Hezekiah, a 'good' king.

Pekah: King of Israel 737–732BC. Allied himself to King Rezin of Syria in opposition to the Assyrians, and put pressure on Jotham and his successor Ahaz to join them. Because they did not join him, Pekah moved in force against Jerusalem, which was unsuccessfully besieged (Isaiah 7:1; compare 2 Kings 15—16).

Remnant: The fortunate few who are promised a return to Jerusalem after exile. The term is subsequently used also for an inward spiritual 'return' to God in faith or repentance. Thus, in Second Isaiah the remnant of Israel is a holy group of survivors, the post-exilic community.

Rezin: King of Syria (Damascus), who, in alliance with Pekah of Israel (Samaria), threatened Ahaz of Judah (Isaiah 7:1; 2 Kings 15:37; 16:5).

Syria: The nation to the north of Israel/Judah, also called Aram.

Torah: The Hebrew term for God's 'law' or 'instruction', often used to refer to the foundational first five books of the Bible as a whole.

Uzziah: King of Judah 769–741BC. Immediately following Uzziah's reign, Isaiah received his call (Isaiah 6:1).

YHWH: The particular name for God, given to Moses at the time of his calling to lead the Israelites out of Egypt (Exodus 3:14–15; 6:2–3). It is associated with God's rescue of his people at the exodus and his making of a covenant with them at Sinai (Exodus 19:3–8). Because of uncertainty as to how to pronounce the divine name, given that the Hebrew consists of four consonants, Jews tend to say 'Adonai' (literally, 'my Lord'), from which the vowels are sometimes borrowed to vocalize the name as YaHoWaH or 'Jehovah'.

Zion: Geographically, this refers to the 'mountain' in Jerusalem on which was built the temple. Theologically, it is used to refer to the place where God is understood to dwell and the place from which he reigns. In Isaiah, a 'Zion theology' develops, according to which the nations will gather one day at Zion to worship God. Because of God's promises concerning Zion, Judah (naively) assumed that God would protect the well-being of Jerusalem unconditionally, but this proved not to be the case.

NOTES

NOTES

NOTES

NOTES

NOTES

NOTES

NOTES

ISAIAH

THE PEOPLE'S
BIBLE COMMENTARY

VOUCHER SCHEME

The People's Bible Commentary (PBC) provides a range of readable, accessible commentaries that will grow into a library covering the whole Bible.

To help you build your PBC library, we have a voucher scheme that works as follows: a voucher is printed on this page of each People's Bible Commentary volume (as above). These vouchers count towards free copies of other books in the series.

For every four purchases of PBC volumes you are entitled to a further volume FREE.

Please find the coupon for the PBC voucher scheme opposite.

All you need do:

- Cut out the vouchers from the PBCs you have purchased and attach them to the coupon.

- Complete your name and address details, and indicate your choice of free book from the list on page 208.

- Take the coupon to your local Christian bookshop who will exchange it for your free PBC book; or send the coupon straight to BRF who will send you your free book direct. Please allow 28 days for delivery.

Please note that PBC volumes provided under the voucher scheme are subject to availability. If your first choice is not available, you may be sent your second choice of book.

THE PEOPLE'S
BIBLE COMMENTARY

VOUCHER SCHEME COUPON

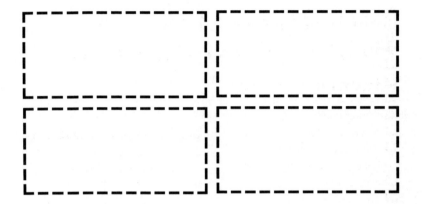

Customer and bookseller should both complete the form overleaf.

Name: . . . .

Address: . . . .

. . . .

Postcode: . . . .

My choice of free PBC volume is:
(Please indicate a first and second choice;
all volumes are supplied subject to
availability.)

❏ Genesis
❏ Exodus
❏ Leviticus and Numbers
❏ Deuteronomy
❏ Joshua and Judges
❏ Ruth, Esther, Ecclesiastes,
  Song of Songs, Lamentations
❏ 1 & 2 Samuel
❏ 1 & 2 Kings
❏ Chronicles to Nehemiah
❏ Job
❏ Psalms 1—72
❏ Psalms 73—150
❏ Proverbs
❏ Isaiah
❏ Jeremiah
❏ Ezekiel
❏ Daniel
❏ Hosea to Micah
❏ Nahum to Malachi
❏ Matthew
❏ Mark
❏ Luke
❏ John
❏ Acts
❏ Romans
❏ 1 Corinthians
❏ 2 Corinthians
❏ Galatians and Thessalonians

❏ Ephesians to Colossians
  and Philemon
❏ Timothy, Titus and Hebrews
❏ James to Jude
❏ Revelation